HOB

HOB

a simpler way to cook:
80 stove-top recipes
for everyone

amy
sheppard

with photography by
polly webster

BLOOMSBURY ABSOLUTE

LONDON · OXFORD · NEW YORK · NEW DELHI · SYDNEY

contents

introduction

introduction

Last year, just a few days after Christmas, my oven stopped working. I was right in the middle of cooking dinner. It wasn't the end of the world. A simple fix, just a part that needed replacing, but it was out of action for a week.

To be honest, the relief I felt that the oven didn't break two days earlier (in the middle of Christmas dinner) eclipsed any annoyance I might have felt. And I still had the hob...

I wrote a new meal plan and spent the week cooking exclusively on the hob. I loved it. It got me out of my cooking rut and forced me to strip everything back. I tried new foods and new ways of cooking and simplified the old. I also discovered a few things. The first thing I discovered is that hob cooking is more forgiving. There's more flexibility than there is with oven cooking. There's time to make mistakes. The window of cooking food to perfection is much wider.

Yes, hob cooking can be slow – in fact I've written a whole chapter on it – but, as you'll see from this book, it's generally a much quicker, simpler way of cooking. Immediately you're eliminating the 15-minute wait to 'pre-heat the oven'. You're cooking on heat straight away.

I've provided a rough guide as to how long each recipe might take you to cook (not including prep), to help you plan ahead, but I'm aware that everyone's hob may be a little different, and sometimes it can depend on the ingredients you're using, so it might take you a little longer in some cases.

I found that hob cooking can be much more conducive to busy lives and family dinner times. It's right there, simmering, sautéing or frying in front of you. Speed it up, slow it down, reheat it. Perfect if you have a chaotic, multi-functioning kitchen like mine.

I wanted to write a cook book that I would want to use. So, I've structured this book so that it fits easily with meal planning. Whether you're short of time, short of money, entertaining friends or looking for something for the weekend – you'll be able to find a Hob meal for you.

There are seven chapters. Some recipes will need a side, like rice or potatoes, so you'll need two pans. However, two-thirds of the recipes are one-pan meals. There are icons at the top of each recipe to indicate whether or not it's a one-pan or two-pan meal.

Does it matter what type of hob you have? No. Gas, electric, induction, it doesn't matter. The only temperature directions are low, medium or high. You know your hob; you know how fast or slow it cooks. These recipes will give you the flexibility to cook more intuitively.

lunch & brunch Full of quick meals and snacks, this chapter brims with the sort of food you can cook on a lazy Saturday morning and eat in bed with the papers.

quick dinners Exactly what the title tells you: quick and simple meals, with easy prep and few ingredients, and on the table in less than 20 minutes. These are easy wins that are ideal for busy, midweek evenings.

weekend food This chapter is all about fakeaways, treats and exciting ingredients. Guilty pleasures that are perfect for weekends when you want something a little bit special.

budget wonders I love having a few cheap recipes up my sleeve. When you're on a budget and need to make your food go even further, you need ideas on how to make something great from the basics. Think tinned, frozen and cheap ingredients with simple ways to use leftovers.

a low simmer These dinners will take a little bit longer. They are meals to cook for pleasure, when you have the time to really enjoy the process. Think stews, casseroles and comfort food. It's slow cooking to get incredible flavours out of great ingredients.

midweek crowd pleasers A chapter of dinners that will become your weekly regulars, these are band new family favourites that you'll hopefully end up knowing off by heart.

sweet hob I nearly didn't include a pudding chapter in this book. I wasn't sure if there were enough desserts that you can make on the hob – I was wrong! I've written some quick and easy sweet treats that I think will become firm family favourites.

simple sides A few ideas for quick accompaniments to any meal.

I really hope you enjoy #HOB. If you make any of the recipes, don't forget to tag me @amysheppardfood – I love seeing what you're cooking!

Amy x

kitchen kit

I don't have a big selection of kitchen kit. In fact, most of the pots and pans I own I've had for many years; some were even my grandparents'. I like to stick to what I know when I'm cooking. I have pans that get hotter than others, some that retain their heat better than others and some that have excellent non-stick credentials!

My point is, that you don't need any fancy kit to make the recipes in this book. Anything that you don't have, there'll be an alternative.

pots & pans

As a guide, though, below I've outlined the main pans you'll need to cook the recipes in this book:

a casserole pan A large, deep, heavy-bottomed, two-handled casserole pan. These are often copper or cast iron.

▶ Cast iron is perfect for slow cooking. It takes a while to heat up, but once hot, it stays hot. Remember, then, the food inside will continue to cook a while after you've turned the heat off.

▶ Copper pans are expensive, but most will last a lifetime if you look after them. They heat quickly and more evenly than cast iron and cool down just as fast. The responsiveness of these pans is what makes them a favourite with chefs.

▶ Use a casserole pan primarily for slow cooking. Ideally, choose one with a non-stick base to make braising easier. If it's an old faithful with little non-stick left, don't worry. You'll use it mainly for cooking casseroles, stews and soups. If you don't have one, just use a standard saucepan.

a non-stick frying pan Choose a frying pan that has an excellent non-stick bottom – which you'll need for some of the recipes. In fact, this is the only bit of kitchen kit that I replace every couple of years as the bottom becomes tired and food begins to stick. Some of the recipes require a frying pan with a lid. Don't worry if you don't have one – all the recipes have been tested using a substitute. You can use a sauté pan or shallow casserole pan with a lid if you have one. Or, you can carefully cover the top of the pan with foil or the bottom of a metal baking tray – basically, anything that stops steam escaping.

a medium, non-stick saucepan with lid This is your standard saucepan. These tend to be either stainless steal or aluminium with a non-stick coating. If you're using a stainless-steel pan, food can sometimes stick. Try using a little more oil and turning down the heat. I have a saucepan with a spout that you can pour from when the lid is still on. It allows you to drain pasta and vegetables without using a colander – a game changer as far as saucepans are concerned!

There are a number of different types of hob. Electric, gas, induction – each with their advantages and disadvantages. I won't run you through the benefits of each one as chances are you've either selected the right one for you, or you've inherited it with the house. Either way, you'll probably know it like the back of your hand.

and what of the hob?

You can make all the recipes in this book with any type of hob. The instructions will guide you to use low, medium or high heat settings and, sometimes, whether you should use a large or small burner. One of the benefits of cooking on the hob is that you can see the food as it's frying, simmering or steaming. This makes cooking on the hob a more intuitive experience. If your food is cooking too fast, turn the heat down; too slowly – crank it up a bit.

modern meal planning

All the recipes in this book have been made in my kitchen and tested multiple times, often at chaotic family dinners. Any recipes that were stressful to make, overly complicated or that I just didn't enjoy cooking, did not make the book. I wanted the recipes to be easy and joyful to make – think dinners that you'll make over and over and recommend to your friends. I also wanted the chapters and recipes to fit in easily with meal planning. If you've not meal planned before, or you're looking for a new way to do it, there is no better way to save time and money, so read on.

I promise you that 10 minutes a week of writing down what dinners you're having, and when, will change dinner times (and your budget) for the better – for ever. Meal planning will:

▶ Help you prepare for busier nights.

▶ Mean you waste less food. Every ingredient that you buy will be allocated to a meal.

▶ Spend less money on your weekly food bill. You'll only buy the food you need.

▶ Mean you spend less time having to cobble together dinners from a random selection of food and more time cooking the food you love.

There is a reason that recipe-box companies have been such an overnight success. We all want to cook, but we want it to be simple, we need it to fit in with our busy lives and, ultimately, we want a plan.

I've organised the recipes and created the chapters in the book with the aim of making meal planning easier for you. Follow these simple steps and hopefully you'll find plenty of recipes to inspire your weekly plan and get the DIY recipe-box experience:

1 Every two or three months write a 'Master Meal Plan.' Don't worry, it sounds more complicated than it is. This is a list of all the regular dinners that you cook, plus a few new ones. You'll need 20 to 25 dinners on this list. It seems like a lot, but once you get started, you'll realise how many you already have in your armoury. Once you run out of the obvious mealtime hits, think back to dinners you've not had in a while and get ideas from the rest of the family.

2 Once you have the list, you need to split it into categories with four or five recipes in each:

quick dinners These are the meals that take about 20 minutes to get on the table. There's a whole chapter of ideas in this book (see pages 47-73). Don't forget to add the simple dinners. Meals like jacket potatoes and beans on toast are a vital part of any meal plan!

budget Think tinned food, cheap ingredients and dinners that use up leftovers like vegetables (soups and stir fries) and mashed potato (fishcakes, bubble and squeak, topping for cottage pie). Take a look at the budget chapter for ideas (see pages 101–127).

weekend food These are the treat dinners: pizza, fish and chips, fakeaways. They're your weekly guilty pleasures and long-cook Sunday lunches. Take inspiration from the Weekend Food and A Low Simmer chapters in this book (see pages 75–99 and 129–153, respectively).

family favourites Or as I've called them, Midweek Crowd Pleasers (see pages 155–181). Put your midweek regulars in this category: the family staples. Fajitas, spaghetti bolognese, tacos, meatballs and lasagne are a few of our favourites.

something new If you're anything like me, you'll probably have a collection of recipes that you want to try; recipes you've found in cookbooks, or online or in magazines. Now's your chance to try them.

3 Once you have your recipes in order, you're ready to write your weekly meal plan. Write down the seven days of the week (or make it repeat to give ten or 14 days if you prefer to shop for longer):

▶ Fill in Saturday and Sunday with dinners from Weekend Food and A Low Simmer.

▶ Identify which one or two nights of the week will be busiest for you. These might be nights where you're working late, or maybe the kids have swimming lessons. Select meals from Quick Dinners.

Shopping List.
- Coriander.
- Paprika.
- Lemons.

▶ Select one or two of the meals from Budget. Cooking at least one budget meal a week will keep the cost of your shop down. If it's the week before pay day or you're cutting back, choose more than just one or two.

▶ Fill in the remaining days of the week from your list of family favourites and try adding one of the meals from your list of something new.

4 Once you have your weekly meal plan, work down the list of dinners. Write down all the ingredients you'll need on your shopping list.

Other things you might want to consider when meal planning:

▶ Have at least one meat-free dinner a week.

▶ Think about adding some lunches. There are plenty of ideas in the Lunch & Brunch chapter (see pages 23–45).

▶ Try, if you can, to select some recipes that share some of the same ingredients. It will reduce the amount of food you have to buy and minimise waste.

▶ Change the Master Meal Plan every two or three months – after all, by then new recipes may very well have become family favourites!

▶ Add a couple of dessert recipes from the Sweet chapter (see page 183–207) – if not for during the week, then certainly as a treat at the weekend.

If you're a little overwhelmed by the number of steps I've included to create a meal plan – don't be. Once you start, meal planning is incredibly easy. With your Master Meal Plan in your pocket, you'll never look back!

To make meal planning a little easier, I've added a few weekly meal plan templates to the back of this book, with space to write your shopping list. There's a few, so you'll be able to create a number of different variations to keep things interesting!

the hob pantry

The following isn't an exhaustive list, but it is a list of some of my favourite storecupboard ingredients. These are additions that can turn a good meal into a great meal; food items that you might not necessarily think to keep in your cupboards and tips on how to use them.

balsamic vinegar I always have this in the cupboard. I add it to sauce bases. It helps to balance the sharpness of tomato. Use it to make simple salad dressings by adding it to equal quantities of oil. From this you can add any spices, seasoning or flavour that you like.

breadcrumbs If you're anything like me, you'll nearly always have a leftover crust of bread hanging around. Blitz any bread past its best to breadcrumbs and freeze them. They defrost quickly and are great for bulking out burgers, coating chicken or fishcakes, and frying to put on top of pasta or salad dishes.

chipotle chilli powder If you're a fan of hot, smoked barbecue flavours, you need a jar of this in your spice cupboard. Experiment by swapping regular chilli powder for this in some of your recipes. It adds a different type of heat and makes a nice change.

coconut milk This is such a useful staple. I use coconut milk in fish stews, curries, soups and sauces. It's a very kid-friendly ingredient – you can even use it for breakfast in smoothies or overnight oats. The coconut flavour isn't strong, you just get a nice, creamy, background sweetness.

crème fraîche If this isn't a regular on your shopping list, it should be. Use it in pasta sauces, casseroles, curries and chicken dishes. You don't need very much to add a creamy silkiness to sauces.

frozen spinach I rarely buy fresh spinach these days. It's expensive and there's only a short time when it's at its best before going soggy. Having spinach in the freezer means I have it whenever I need it – you soon realise that it's a nice addition to a lot of dinners.

garam masala I feel like this is an underrated spice blend. It's full of wonderful, warming flavours, without being spicy. If you're introducing children to curries or cooking for people who don't like their food too spicy, this is a great way to go.

gouda cheese I buy this cheese in slices. It melts quickly without being too fatty and gives you a lovely gooey, stringy cheese when cooked, making it perfect for toasties and sauces.

gravy granules I use beef and chicken gravy granules (depending on the meat I'm using) in casseroles, pies and even chilli con carne. It helps to thicken the sauce and gives a deeper flavour to the meat.

halloumi If you're trying to eat less meat, halloumi is a wonderful vegetarian ingredient. It has great texture and flavour and is incredibly versatile. Coat it in a little flour and fry until golden to add to salads. Coat in breadcrumbs for lovely croutons to add to soups and pasta dishes; or use it in vegetable curries.

honey We seem to get through quite a lot of honey in my house. I often swap sugar for honey in midweek recipes – usually in tomato-based dinners that require a bit of sweetness to balance out the flavour, like spaghetti bolognese and lasagne.

jalapeño slices I always have a jar of these in the fridge and it's surprising how often I use them. I love the vinegary pickled heat. They are great in wraps, burgers and salads or cut up finely and added to mayonnaise.

red pesto Most people have green pesto at the back of the cupboard, but red pesto doesn't seem to be as popular. It's a great addition to any tomato-based pasta sauce, pizza topping, burger mixture, or anything that would benefit from a good kick of sundried tomato.

rice noodles These are lighter than normal noodles, gluten-free and cook in 2 minutes. Add them straight to soups and stir fries to quickly bulk out one-pan meals.

rice pouches I use these all the time, they're so convenient. The rice is already cooked, so needs only a few minutes to heat through. They are great for quick lunches or adding straight to curries and stews for easy one-pot wonders!

sourdough I often have sourdough in the freezer. I cut up a loaf and store a few slices in a freezer bag. Its solid structure and firm texture make it great for toasties, croutons, pizza bread and soups.

soy sauce Soy sauce isn't just for stir fries. Use it in salad dressings, curry bases and marinades. It goes well with fish and with honey, garlic and chilli. If you have a recipe that calls for fish sauce, you can happily swap it for soy.

spring greens This large-leafed often tatty-looking veg is always on my shopping list. It's cheap, it lasts for ages and has great texture. Finely slice it into ribbons and sauté it – it's a great swap for spinach and perfect for soups and stews.

squeezy mixed herbs If you've not bought these before, they're the herbs you get in a tube. They're preserved in a vinaigrette – think mint sauce but with mixed herbs. It's a great way to quickly add flavour to dishes. They keep for a long time, which saves on buying lots of packet herbs that don't keep for long.

tinned fish Many people have tins of tuna and salmon in the cupboard, but mackerel and sardines are less popular. They're both great ingredients. Mackerel is a brilliant addition to rice and potato dishes and is perfectly matched with curried flavours and other hot spices. Sardines love parsley, garlic, lemon and buttery flavours – so get experimenting!

tinned potatoes Tinned potatoes have come a long way, so discard any ill feeling you might have towards them! Add them to stews and curries, pan-fry them as a quick side, or heat them through with melted butter and herbs.

lunch & brunch

This chapter is full of simple recipes that will turn brunch time on its head. From exciting new ways with eggs to next-level wraps, prep-ahead packed lunches and quick snacks, these are recipes to brighten up your Sunday mornings and liven up Tuesday lunchtimes.

perfect poached eggs & devilled crumpets

You might be surprised to see a poached-egg recipe in this cook book. I've seen so many recipes for poached eggs over the years, all requiring a complicated technique or a bit of kit. I wanted to share my recipe that will give you perfect eggs every time and will put 'poachies' firmly back on the lunchtime menu. The curried crumpets are ideal with the egg. If you don't want them spicy, just fry them in butter. Wilted spinach is a nice addition to this dish too.

makes 2 | 10min

30g butter
1 teaspoon curry powder
2 crumpets
1 teaspoon white wine
   vinegar
2 eggs
salt and freshly ground
   black pepper

1 First, prepare the crumpets. Melt the butter in a non-stick frying pan on a medium heat. When bubbling, reduce the heat to low, stir in the curry powder and leave to cook for 1 minute.

2 Add the crumpets to the pan, turning them over and pressing down until they're coated in butter. Increase the heat to medium and fry for 5 minutes, turning them over every minute or so, or until crisp on the top and bottom. Press them down occasionally to ensure they're cooked through.

3 While the crumpets are cooking, half fill a large saucepan with water. Add the teaspoon of white wine vinegar and bring the water to a furious boil.

4 Carefully break 1 egg into a ladle or large serving spoon. Turn off the heat for the water and leave for a few seconds to become still.

5 Lower the egg into the water and quickly tip it from the ladle or spoon in one swift movement.

6 With the heat still turned off, leave the egg for 3½ minutes (set a timer). Add another egg in the same way exactly 1 minute after the first went in. The water will still be hot enough and timing will be easier.

7 Carefully remove the first egg from the pan with a slotted spoon, holding it over the pan for a few seconds to drain any excess water. A minute later, remove the second. Use scissors to trim any loose bits of egg white. Serve the eggs on top of the crumpets, seasoned with a pinch of salt and black pepper.

egg & bacon breakfast wrap

This is the perfect brunch (or breakfast) on the go. It's filling and tasty and you can add whatever topping you like. I've used avocado, but tomato, mushrooms, fried onion and cooked sausages are all good accompaniments, too.

makes 1 | **15**min

olive oil, for frying
2 rashers of smoked
 back bacon
2 eggs
1 tablespoon whole milk
1 flour tortilla
½ avocado, sliced,
 to serve
salt and freshly ground
 black pepper

1 Drizzle a little oil into a non-stick frying pan with a base the size of a tortilla, and place it on a medium heat. Add the bacon and fry for 5 minutes, turning a couple of times, until crisp. Remove from the pan and set aside.

2 Beat the eggs with the milk and season with a little salt and pepper.

3 Brush the remaining bacon fat around the pan and pour in the egg. Roll the egg around, so that the bottom of the pan is covered, to make an omelette. Fry on a medium heat for a minute or two, until the egg is cooked on the underside (it should slide easily around the pan once you've loosened the edges). Flip the omelette over and cook for 1–2 minutes on the other side, until golden.

4 Place a tortilla on top of the cooked omelette.

5 Place the palm of your hand on top of the tortilla and invert the pan to turn out the contents on to your hand (alternatively, invert directly on to a plate). Slide the tortilla and omelette back into the pan so that the tortilla is now on the bottom.

6 Fry for 2 minutes, until the tortilla starts to crisp.

7 Arrange the slices of bacon in the middle of the egg and lay the avocado slices over the top. Slide the tortilla on to a plate and fold in the sides to serve.

cowboy beans

There's something really satisfying about making your own baked beans. It's incredibly easy and they keep for several days in the fridge. I've put this in the lunch chapter, but often this is a dinner for us. Serve it on the garlic ciabatta on page 106 and add a poached egg (see page 24).

feeds 4-6 | 25min

olive oil, for frying
1 onion, finely chopped
1 roasted red pepper
  from a jar, cut into
  slivers
1 tablespoon runny honey
1 tablespoon balsamic
  vinegar
2 teaspoons smoked
  paprika
pinch of mild or hot chilli
  (depending on how spicy
  you like it)
2 x 400g tins of haricot
  beans, drained
500g passata
salt and freshly ground
  black pepper

to serve (optional)
slices of toast
poached eggs (see
  page 24)
small handful of
  coriander, finely
  chopped

1   Drizzle a little oil into a large saucepan on a medium heat. Add the onion and fry for 5 minutes, until softened.

2   Add the red pepper, honey, balsamic vinegar, paprika and chilli powder. Fry for 2 minutes, then stir in the beans and passata, and season with salt and pepper. Bring to the boil, then turn the heat down and simmer for 15 minutes, stirring regularly.

3   Serve the beans on toast - I like mine topped with a poached egg, scattered with a little coriander and finished with a few extra grindings of black pepper.

tip: Want to make this really special? Add some smoked bacon lardons or finely sliced chorizo to the onions before frying.

smoky bean shakshuka

This version of a shakshuka has the welcome addition of beans to make it really substantial. A classic brunch dish, serve it on toast and you've got an easy midweek dinner option, too. You'll need a frying or sauté pan with a lid to ensure the egg cooks through. If you don't have one, just carefully cover the pan with foil.

feeds 4 | 30min

olive oil, for frying
1 onion, finely sliced
1 red pepper, deseeded and finely sliced
1 garlic clove, finely chopped
1 teaspoon ground cumin
½–1 teaspoon hot or mild chilli powder (depending on how spicy you like it)
1 teaspoon runny honey
1 heaped teaspoon smoked paprika
1 x 400g tin of baked beans
1 x 400g tin of mixed beans, drained
300g passata
4 eggs
small handful of coriander, finely chopped, to serve
salt and freshly ground black pepper

1 Drizzle a little oil into a large, deep frying pan with a lid, and place on a medium heat. Add the onion and pepper and fry (without the lid) for 5 minutes, until the onion is softened.

2 Add the garlic, cumin, chilli powder, honey and paprika to the pan and fry for a further 1 minute.

3 Stir in both tins of beans and the passata, then season with salt and pepper. Simmer for 10 minutes, stirring occasionally, until the mixture thickens enough that you can make little indentations in it with the back of a spoon. Check the sauce is spicy enough for you and adjust the seasoning as required.

4 Use the back of the spoon to make a well in the mixture. Quickly and carefully break 1 egg into the well. Sprinkle with a little salt and pepper and repeat for the remaining eggs, making sure they're well spaced out.

5 Turn the heat down to low, place the lid on the pan or cover with foil and leave for about 7 minutes or until the whites of the egg are cooked and the yolks have a light film over them. Serve immediately sprinkled with chopped coriander and with slices of good, buttered toast.

halloumi & sundried tomato toastie

This is the ultimate lunchtime treat! Crisp, salty halloumi with a creamy red pesto mayo and a peppery kick from the rocket. It takes about 15 minutes to make, so not the quickest of lunches, but definitely worth the effort!

makes 1 toastie | 15min

2 tablespoons plain flour
pinch of mild chilli powder
¼ teaspoon freshly
  ground black pepper,
  plus extra to season
4 thick slices of halloumi
  cheese
olive oil, for frying
2 thick slices of white
  bread
1 tablespoon mayonnaise
1 heaped teaspoon red
  pesto
handful of rocket leaves

1   Place the flour in a small bowl and combine it with the chilli powder and pepper.

2   One at a time, lay each slice of halloumi in the flour mixture, turning it over until it has a light coating.

3   Drizzle a little oil into a large, non-stick frying pan on a medium heat. When hot, add the coated sliced halloumi and fry for 2 minutes on each side, until golden brown but still soft. Remove from the pan and set aside.

4   Heat a little more oil in the pan. When hot, place the slices of bread in the pan, pressing them down gently for 30 seconds until lightly crisp on one side. (You may need to do this one at a time, depending on the size of your pan.) Set aside.

5   Mix together the mayonnaise and red pesto and season with black pepper.

6   Spread the mayonnaise mixture equally over the 2 toasted sides of the bread slices, spreading evenly right up to the edges, as if you were buttering toast.

7   On one of the slices, lay over the halloumi slices, then place the other slice, spread-side downwards on top, to create a sandwich. Fry the sandwich on a medium-low heat for 1-2 minutes on each side, until golden brown and crisp.

8   Remove from the pan, carefully open the toastie and add a handful of rocket leaves. Close the toastie again, halve and serve.

tuna quesadillas

Quesadillas are a great way to use up tortillas, especially if they're a little past their best. Of course, you can use whatever filling you like, but the one I've suggested here makes use of simple cupboard ingredients that are really kid friendly.

makes 3 | 20min

2 x 145g tins of tuna in
   spring water, drained
1 dessertspoon
   mayonnaise
2 teaspoons green pesto
roasted red pepper from
   a jar, equivalent to 1 red
   pepper, finely chopped
2 dessertspoons drained
   tinned sweetcorn
6 large flour tortillas
   (24cm diameter)
150g mature cheddar
   cheese, grated
olive oil, for frying
cherry tomatoes, halved
   or whole, and salad
   leaves, to serve
salt and freshly ground
   black pepper

1   Mix the tuna, mayonnaise, pesto, pepper and sweetcorn together and season with salt and pepper.

2   Divide the mixture equally between 3 flour tortillas, spreading the filling right up to the edges. Cover each with a good sprinkling of grated cheese, then place the remaining tortillas on top, like a sandwich.

3   Heat a small amount of oil in a non-stick frying pan over a medium heat. One at a time, fry the quesadillas for 2-3 minutes on each side, until the tortillas are crisp and golden and the cheese has melted. Cut them into wedges and serve with a few cherry tomatoes and some salad leaves (rocket is nice), on the side.

tip: My family love chicken, stuffing and veg quesadillas - basically, whatever's left over from the Sunday roast. Spaghetti bolognese is always a crowd pleasing filling, and a perfect way to make leftovers go further. As long as you top with cheese, you can fill them with whatever you like!

broccoli, potato & stilton soup

I love this soup. It has a thick, silky texture and you can taste the stilton without it overpowering the broccoli. Serve it with bread and butter and it becomes filling enough to pass as a dinner.

feeds 4 | 30min

olive oil, for frying
1 onion, roughly chopped
1 head of broccoli, broken into florets
1.2 litres vegetable stock
300g new or baby potatoes, skin on and halved
120g stilton, crumbled, plus extra to serve
salt and freshly ground black pepper

1 Drizzle a little oil into a large non-stick saucepan with a lid, and place on a medium heat. Add the onion and broccoli and fry (without the lid) for 5 minutes, stirring occasionally, until the onion is softened.

2 Add the stock and potatoes. Place the lid on the pan and simmer on a low heat for 20 minutes, or until the potatoes are tender.

3 Remove the pan from the heat and, using a hand blender, blitz the soup until you have a smooth consistency. Add the stilton, and season with salt and pepper. Stir until the cheese has melted.

4 Ladle into warmed bowls, then top with a little extra black pepper and a small amount of crumbled stilton and a drizzle of oil to serve.

tip: If you don't like stilton, swap it for grated mature cheddar to give you that flavour hit. Alternatively, you can stir in 2 tablespoons spreadable mature cheddar for a cheesy flavour and a more creamy texture.

lemony sardine quinoa

This a really easy, really healthy, really quick lunch. You'll find a few versions of quinoa pouches available in the shops – I use one with added seeds, which gives a nice crunch, but any will do. Or, use a pouch of cooked brown rice, if you prefer.

feeds 2 | 10min

*1 x 120g tin of sardines
   in oil
1 onion, finely sliced
large handful of pre-
   shredded kale (discard
   any thick, tough stems)
1 x 250g pouch of cooked
   quinoa (or rice; or
   a mixture)
juice of ½ lemon
pinch of chilli flakes
   (optional)
salt and freshly ground
   black pepper*

1   Place a drizzle of oil from the sardine tin into a non-stick saucepan on a medium heat. Add the onion and kale and fry for 5 minutes, stirring regularly, until the onion is softened.

2   Add the sardines to the pan and gently break them up with a wooden spoon. Stir in the quinoa or rice, straight from the pouch, breaking it up with the back of a wooden spoon. Stir on a medium heat for about 3 minutes, until all the grains are separated. Add the lemon juice, stir and fry for a further 1 minute to heat through.

3   Season with salt and pepper, and with a sprinkle of chilli flakes if you want a bit of heat.

tip: You can eat this cold, making it a great prep-ahead lunch for work or busy days, so double up the ingredients and you'll thank yourself the next day!

15-minute falafels

These are a simple, throw-together version of a falafel. They're a bit smaller than most falafels so they fry quickly and stay moist. Don't be tempted to use a food processor – the joy of these is that they have a bit of texture. I serve them on flat breads or in wraps, with hummus, tomato, cucumber and jalapeños – a combination inspired by many wonderful lunches with my lovely friend Cass.

makes 4 wraps | 15min

1 x 400g tin of chickpeas
1-2 garlic cloves, finely
    chopped
small handful of
    coriander, finely
    chopped
1 teaspoon ground
    turmeric
1 teaspoon ground cumin
½ teaspoon mild or hot
    chilli powder (depending
    on how spicy you like it)
vegetable or sunflower
    oil, for frying
handful of plain flour
salt and freshly ground
    black pepper

to serve (optional)
4 flat breads or flour
    tortillas
4 level dessertspoons
    hummus
¼ cucumber, diced
8 cherry tomatoes, halved
    or quartered
10 slices of jalapeño from
    a jar, halved

1   First drain the chickpeas. Take the lid off the tin and carefully cover the open top with your hand. Tip the tin upside down over a sink, with your hand still in place. Allow the chickpea water to drain through your fingers.

2   When the water is drained, place the chickpeas in a mixing bowl. Do not rinse. Draining the chickpeas this way will ensure they are still coated in plenty of chickpea water which will help to bind the falafel.

3   Using the end of a rolling pin, crush the chickpeas into a thick, firm paste. This will take a couple of minutes. When the chickpeas are smooth, stir in the garlic, coriander and spices. Use your hands to squash the ingredients together, spreading them evenly as you go. Season generously with salt and pepper.

4   Heat a small drizzle of oil in a large, non-stick frying pan on a high heat until hot. While the oil is heating, roll the falafel mixture into 10 equal-sized balls. Press each piece firmly together before rolling it in the palms of your hands. Roll each ball in the flour, so they are lightly covered.

5   When the oil is spitting hot, add the falafels to the pan. Fry for 5-7 minutes, until golden brown with a crispy shell. Use a dessertspoon to carefully turn them over every 30 seconds-1 minute. They will become more robust as they crisp up. Remove from the pan and set aside to cool for 3-5 minutes. This will help them to firm up.

6   Spread each flat bread or tortilla with hummus. Break each falafel in half and place on top, then scatter over the diced cucumber, chopped tomato and sliced jalapeños. Finish with a little more black pepper, then serve open for the flat breads or rolled for the tortillas.

ham & cheese croissant pudding

It was impossible to come up with a good name for this one! It's basically a simple, savoury version of a bread and butter pudding. If you want to make it veggie, just leave out the ham – it's still a great-tasting combination.

feeds 3–4 | 15min

3–4 small croissants
   (depending on the size
   of your pan)
3–4 slices of baked ham
3–4 slices of gouda or
   mature cheddar cheese
30g butter
3 eggs
100ml whole milk
salt and freshly ground
   black pepper

1   Slice open the croissants and place a slice of ham and a slice of cheese in each.

2   Close the croissants and firmly press them down with your hands so that they're flat. Cut the filled croissants across their width.

3   Heat the butter in a frying or sauté pan with a lid (or you can use foil). Arrange the croissants so that they're evenly spaced in the pan and fry on a medium heat (lid off for now) for 2 minutes on each side.

4   In the meantime, beat the eggs and milk together, seasoning with a little salt and pepper.

5   Pour the egg mixture around the croissants and place the lid on the pan. If you don't have a lid, carefully cover the pan with foil.

6   Cook for about 7 minutes, adjusting the heat up or down if the egg is cooking too slowly or too fast – it's ready when the egg on top is set. To test: lift the pan and swirl it around a little to see if the egg is still runny. When it's ready, season with a little more black pepper, if you wish, then cut and serve immediately.

tip: This works best with the small, cheap, multi-pack croissants, rather than the larger deluxe ones.

cheese & garlic potato cakes

The key to turning these from good to incredible is to roll them out nice and thinly. That way they'll fry quickly and you get a lovely crust. These make a great lunch served with the Steamed Spinach & Cashews on page 214, or serve them with chicken or fish as a side dish. They freeze well, so make extra. Just put them in the freezer before you fry them. They'll keep in the freezer for up to 3 months.

makes 8 cakes | 30min

800g baking potatoes,
 peeled and cut into
 4–5cm pieces
40g butter, plus a little
 extra for frying
2 garlic cloves, finely
 chopped
80g mature cheddar
 cheese, coarsely grated
80g plain flour, plus extra
 for dusting
small handful of
 coriander, leaves picked,
 to serve
salt and freshly ground
 black pepper

1 Place the potatoes in a large saucepan of salted water. Place the pan on a high heat and bring to the boil. Reduce the heat and simmer for about 15-20 minutes, until the potatoes are tender.

2 Drain the potatoes and allow them to steam off in the colander for a few minutes. Return them to the pan and mash them with a fork, until smooth. Season and leave to cool in the pan.

3 Place the 40g butter in a large non-stick frying pan on a low heat and gently melt. Add the garlic and fry for 2 minutes, until just softened. Pour the garlic butter on to the potatoes (set aside the pan with the oily, garlicky residue) and add the cheese. Mix until evenly combined, then add the flour and mix again to combine.

4 Turn out the potato mixture on to a floured worktop and gently knead until you have a sticky dough. Roughly press the dough into a circle and use a rolling pin to roll out the circle until it's 1cm thick.

5 Cut the dough circle into 8 equal wedges (halve it, quarter it, then halve each quarter).

6 Add a little more butter to the frying pan and place on a high heat until the butter starts to spit. Turn the heat down to medium and fry the potato cakes in batches for 2 minutes on each side, adding more butter when you need it, until they are golden brown all over. Leave to cool for a couple of minutes before serving sprinkled with coriander, if you wish.

tip: Try adding a pinch of chilli for a bit of kick or use gouda instead of cheddar for a gooey, melted centre.

quick dinners

This is your go-to chapter for busy evenings after tiring days. The recipes are dinners that you can get on the table quickly with minimum fuss and few ingredients – think flavour-filled stir fries, speedy curries and crowd-pleasing pasta. They are all the stress-free recipes you'll ever need.

halloumi hash

In my opinion, everything tastes better with halloumi! This recipe uses mainly tinned ingredients, so not only is it quick, it's a good standby.

feeds 4 | 25min

olive oil, for frying
2 x 225g blocks of halloumi, sliced into ½–1cm-thick slices
1 onion, finely sliced
2 red peppers, deseeded and finely sliced
200g tenderstem broccoli, rough ends trimmed
2 x 567g tins of peeled new potatoes, drained and rinsed
2 garlic cloves, finely chopped
1 x 400g tin of chickpeas, drained
1 tablespoon smoked paprika
1 tablespoon tomato purée
2 tablespoons boiling water
salt and freshly ground black pepper

1 Add a small amount of oil to a large, non-stick frying pan on a medium heat. When hot, add the halloumi slices and fry for 7–10 minutes, turning regularly, until golden brown on both sides. Set the halloumi aside.

2 In the same pan add the onion, peppers and broccoli. Add a little more oil, if you need it, and fry on a medium heat for 5 minutes, stirring occasionally, until the onion is softened.

3 Pat the potatoes dry with kitchen roll. Cut each potato in half, then add the halves to the pan along with the garlic, chickpeas and paprika. Fry for 10 minutes on a low heat, stirring regularly and adding more oil if the pan gets too dry, until the vegetables are tender and the potatoes are heated through.

4 Stir in the tomato purée and the boiling water, and season with salt and pepper. Fry for a final 2 minutes, until the potatoes and vegetables are coated. Top with the halloumi and serve straight from the pan.

tip: You can swap the halloumi for goat's cheese, just slice it and place it on the top at the end, rather than frying.

stilton spaghetti with walnut toastie bits

You can get this dinner on the table in just under 15 minutes. The flavours of the blue cheese are quite grown up, so we tend to have this one without the kids. Use your favourite blue cheese – I've used stilton here, but gorgonzola or roquefort are also particularly lovely. If you don't like walnuts, just leave them out to make toastie bits. Not everyone is a fan of kale, so swap this for spinach or savoy cabbage if you prefer.

feeds 2 | 15min

200g dried spaghetti
large handful of pre-
    shredded kale (discard
    the tougher stalks)
20g walnut halves
30g butter
1 slice of bread, roughly
    grated
120g stilton (or other blue
    cheese), crumbled
20ml whole milk
100g crème fraîche
salt and freshly ground
    black pepper

1 Break the spaghetti in half, place in a saucepan and cover with boiling water. Salt the water, place over a high heat and bring to the boil. Reduce the heat and simmer for 6 minutes, then add the shredded kale to the pan and cook for a further 4 minutes, until the spaghetti is cooked and the kale is tender.

2 While the pasta is cooking, make the walnut toastie bits. Roughly crush the walnuts into small pieces with a pestle and mortar or the end of a rolling pin.

3 Melt the butter in a non-stick frying pan on a medium heat. Add the grated bread and the walnut pieces and season with salt and pepper. Toss the crumbs around the pan until they're coated in melted butter. Fry on a medium heat for 3-4 minutes, until toasted. Remove from the pan and set aside.

4 Place the stilton, milk and crème fraîche in the frying pan. Warm through on a medium-low heat, stirring continuously, until the cheese has melted and the sauce is just at boiling point. Season with black pepper.

5 When the pasta and kale are ready, use tongs to lift them from the cooking water straight into the sauce. Any cooking water that clings on to the pasta and greens will help the sauce to combine and thicken. Move the pasta around the pan until it's coated in the sauce.

6 Divide the pasta between 2 bowls. Sprinkle over the walnut toastie bits and season with a little more black pepper to serve.

one-pot veg & feta couscous

This is an easy, midweek dinner option and a great way to use up leftover veg. Sweet potato, butternut squash and aubergine are all great additions or swaps if you have them.

feeds 4 | 25min

olive oil, for frying
1 red pepper, deseeded
 and finely sliced
1 yellow pepper, deseeded
 and finely sliced
1 onion, finely sliced
½ head of broccoli, cut
 into small florets
200g asparagus tips,
 halved lengthways
3 tablespoons red pesto
340ml boiling water
 (or vegetable stock,
 if you prefer)
300g couscous
200g feta cheese, cut
 into 1-2cm cubes
salt and freshly ground
 black pepper

1   Drizzle a little oil into a large saucepan with a lid, and place on a medium-low heat. Add both peppers, and the onion, broccoli and asparagus and fry, with the lid on, for 10 minutes, regularly removing the lid to stir, until the vegetables have softened. (Keep the lid on between stirring to help the larger vegetables to steam properly.)

2   Remove the lid, add the pesto and fry for a further 1 minute. Turn off the heat and pour the boiling water into the pan, followed by the couscous. Season with salt and pepper. Stir once and quickly place the lid on the pan again to trap in the steam.

3   Leave for 5 minutes, then remove the lid and give it a quick stir, replace the lid again and leave for another 5 minutes. Stir in the cubed feta and serve straightaway.

tip: This recipe works well cold, so it's perfect for batch-cooking lunches, summer picnics and as a side dish for barbecues.

salmon teriyaki noodles

You can vary the veg you use in this recipe. Baby corn, mangetout, spring greens, mushrooms and beansprouts would all work well.

feeds 4 | 30min

olive oil, for frying
handful of sugar
  snap peas
1 red pepper, deseeded
  and finely sliced
bunch of spring onions,
  green and white parts
  roughly chopped
1 large carrot, roughly
  grated
250g medium dried
  egg noodles
2 garlic cloves, finely
  chopped
a large thumb-sized piece
  of fresh ginger, peeled
  and finely chopped
1 red chilli, finely sliced,
  plus extra sliced into
  rings to garnish
1 tablespoon honey
2-3 tablespoons dark
  soy sauce
4 skin-on, boneless
  salmon steaks
small handful of
  coriander, finely
  chopped, to serve
  (optional)
salt

1 Drizzle a little oil into a flat-bottomed wok or large frying pan on a medium-high heat. Add the sugar snap peas, red pepper, spring onions and grated carrot and fry for 10 minutes, stirring regularly, until the vegetables are just beginning to soften.

2 In the meantime, place the noodles in a separate saucepan and cover with boiling water. Bring to the boil, then reduce the heat and simmer for 5 minutes, until cooked. Drain and set aside.

3 Add the garlic, ginger, chilli, honey and soy sauce to the wok. Fry for 2 minutes, until the garlic is softened. Using a spoon, remove the vegetables and any sauce from the pan and set aside in a bowl.

4 Heat a little more oil in the pan and turn the heat up to high. When the oil is spitting hot, fry the salmon steaks, skin-sides downwards, for 3 minutes, then turn them over and fry them for a further 2-3 minutes, or until cooked through. You may have to do this in batches, depending on the size of your wok. Remove from the pan and set aside on a plate.

5 Return the vegetables and any sauce to the wok along with the drained noodles. Move the noodles and veg around the pan for a minute or two, until they're combined and heated through.

6 Divide the noodles equally between 4 bowls, top each portion with a salmon steak and season with a little salt. Scatter over the finely chopped herbs to serve, if you wish.

tip: If you want to make this a one-pan meal and even quicker to get on the table, use straight-to-wok noodles.

sweet chilli tomato & prawn orzo

This is a comfort recipe – one to make when you've had a bad day and you're in need of a hug in a bowl. There is something so satisfying and warming about the sweet and spicy flavour of the tomato sauce with the prawns and pasta. Serve it with pitta bread for dipping.

feeds 4 | 25min

olive oil, for frying
1 onion, finely chopped
250g cherry tomatoes, halved
275g cooked and peeled frozen prawns, defrosted
2 garlic cloves, finely chopped
1 tablespoon balsamic vinegar
1 tablespoon tomato ketchup
½–1 teaspoon mild chilli powder
1 teaspoon dark soy sauce
1 teaspoon light brown soft sugar
900ml vegetable stock
300g orzo
small handful of coriander, finely chopped, to serve (optional)
4 pitta breads, to serve (optional)
salt and freshly ground black pepper

1 Drizzle a little oil into a large saucepan with a lid and place on a medium-low heat. Add the onion and fry (without the lid) for 5 minutes, stirring regularly, until the onion is softened. Add the tomatoes and fry for a further 5 minutes, until they start to break down.

2 Stir in the prawns, garlic, balsamic vinegar, ketchup, chilli powder, soy sauce and sugar. Fry for 1 minute, then add the stock, followed by the orzo, and season with salt and pepper. Stir once and bring to a steady boil.

3 Stir again, turn the heat down to low and place the lid on the pan. Simmer for 10 minutes, stirring 3 or 4 times to prevent the orzo sticking, until the orzo is plump and tender. Remove the lid, turn off the heat and leave to rest for 3 minutes. (Or simmer off any excess liquid if you want a thicker sauce.)

4 Divide the orzo equally between 4 bowls and finish with a little chopped coriander, if you wish. Serve with pitta bread if you want to make it more filling.

chicken laksa

feeds 4 | 20min

olive oil, for frying
3 chicken breasts, cut into
    bite-sized pieces
1 red pepper, deseeded
    and finely sliced
bunch of spring onions,
    white and green parts
    roughly chopped
thumb-sized piece of
    fresh ginger, peeled and
    finely chopped
1 red chilli, finely sliced
    into rings
2 garlic cloves, finely
    sliced
1 teaspoon ground
    turmeric
1 teaspoon ground
    coriander
1 tablespoon dark
    soy sauce
800ml chicken stock
1 x 400g tin of full-fat
    coconut milk
200g dried fine rice
    noodles
small handful of
    coriander, roughly
    chopped, to serve
    (optional)
salt and freshly ground
    black pepper

This is my version of a southeast Asian laksa. It is usually fish-based, but using chicken gives it great flavour and texture. This spicy coconut noodle curry is on the table in 20 minutes and is one of the quickest, tastiest dinners on our weekly meal plan.

1   Drizzle a little oil into a large saucepan with a lid, and place on a low heat. Add the chicken and fry for 5 minutes on a medium heat, until it is no longer pink. Remove the chicken from the pan and set aside.

2   Add a little more oil to the pan along with the pepper, spring onions, ginger, chilli and garlic and fry (without the lid) for 5 minutes, until the vegetables have softened. Add the turmeric, ground coriander and soy sauce. Fry for a further 1 minute, then stir in the stock and coconut milk, and season with salt and pepper. Bring to the boil and simmer for 5 minutes.

3   Break the dried noodles into the pan, then stir in the chicken and place the lid on. Simmer for 4 minutes on a low heat, removing the lid to stir occasionally, until the chicken is cooked through.

4   Serve the laksa in bowls, with a little fresh coriander sprinkled over, if you wish.

tip: To make this a fish laksa, use 3 skinless, boneless white fish fillets such as cod or basa instead of chicken. Cut them into bite-sized pieces and add them to the pan at the same time as the pepper and spring onions.

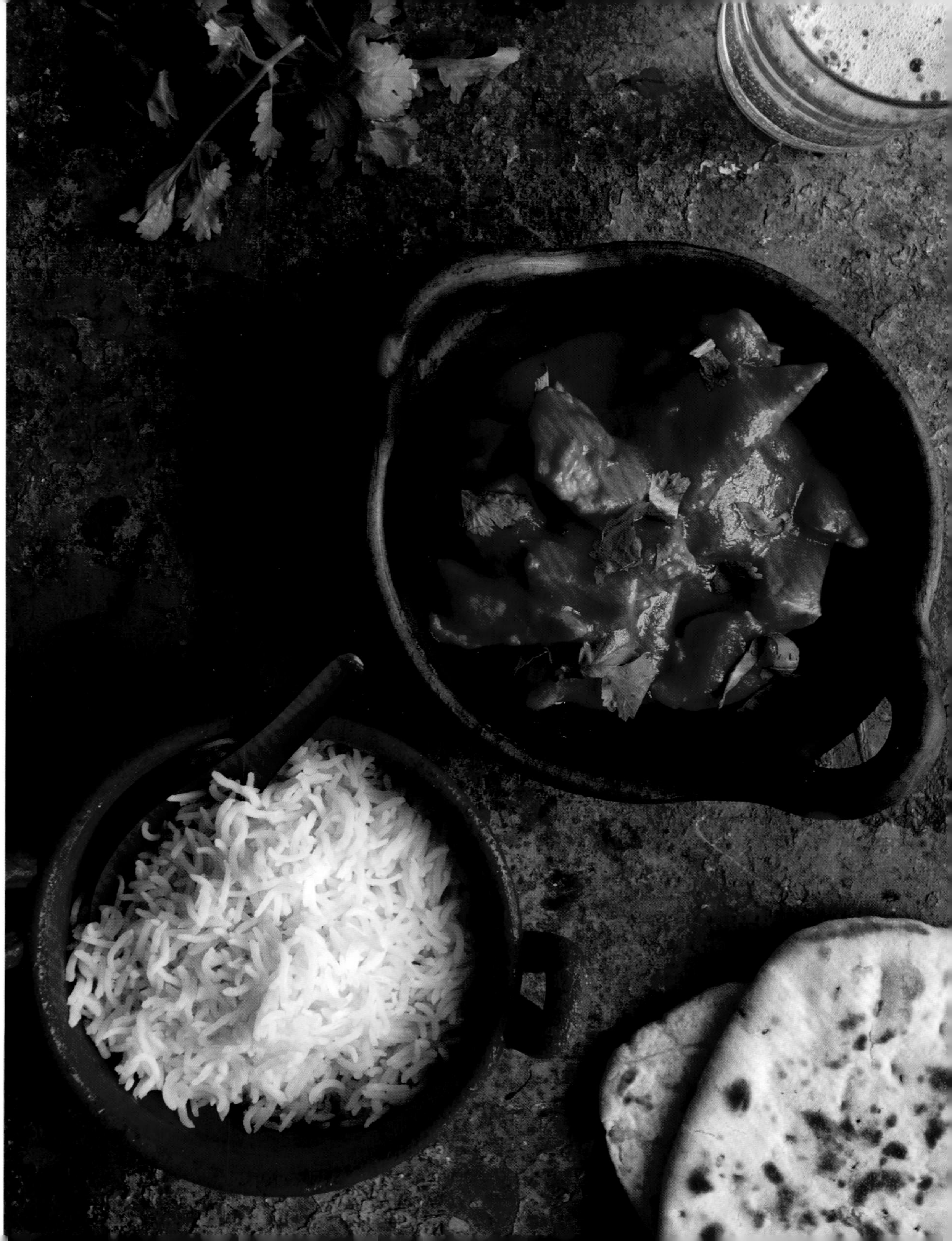

easy butter chicken

The traditional version of this requires you to marinate the chicken overnight and it has considerably more ingredients. This isn't the quickest recipe in the chapter, but the hands-on time is under 10 minutes. It's a fast-cook version of a classic curry, which you can put together with no fuss, even on the busiest of days. This is a two-pan meal if served with rice.

feeds 4–6 | 30min

50g butter
1 onion, finely chopped
750g chicken breast, cut
  into bite-sized pieces
2 tablespoons tomato
  purée
3 garlic cloves, finely
  chopped
1 teaspoon ground ginger
1 teaspoon mild or hot
  chilli powder (depending
  on how spicy you like it)
1 teaspoon paprika
1 teaspoon ground cumin
2 teaspoons garam
  masala
200g passata
1 x 400g tin of full-fat
  coconut milk
boiled white rice and
  naan breads, to serve
small handful of
  coriander, finely
  chopped, to serve
  (optional)
salt and freshly ground
  black pepper

1 Melt the butter in a large saucepan with a lid, on a medium heat. Add the onion and fry (without the lid) for 5 minutes, until the onion has softened. Add the chicken and fry for a further 5 minutes, stirring regularly, until the chicken is no longer pink on the outside.

2 Stir in the tomato purée, garlic, ginger, chilli powder, paprika, cumin and garam masala. Fry for 1–2 minutes, stirring constantly. Stir in the passata and coconut milk, and season with salt and pepper. Bring to a vigorous boil, then turn down the heat to its lowest setting and place the lid on the saucepan.

3 Simmer over a low heat for 15 minutes, or until the chicken is cooked through, and then remove the lid and increase the heat to high to thicken the sauce. Serve with rice and naan bread, and sprinkled with coriander, if you wish.

satay chicken stir-fry

feeds 4 | 25min

olive oil, for frying
500g chicken breast, cut
  into bite-sized pieces
1 red pepper, deseeded
  and finely sliced
5 spring onions, green
  and white parts roughly
  chopped
140g baby corn, halved
  lengthways
large handful of
  mangetout
1 red chilli, finely sliced
  into rings (optional)
150ml full-fat coconut
  milk
1 teaspoon hot chilli
  powder
2 tablespoons smooth
  peanut butter
300g straight-to-wok
  noodles
1 tablespoon lime juice
1 tablespoon soy sauce
small handful of crushed
  unsalted cashew nuts,
  to serve (optional)
small handful of
  coriander, finely
  chopped, to serve
  (optional)
salt and freshly ground
  black pepper

This is a simple, midweek stir-fry with a wonderful, creamy peanut sauce. You don't have to use straight-to-wok noodles – you can boil noodles or use leftover rice, if you prefer.

1   Drizzle a little oil in a wok or large non-stick frying pan on a medium heat. When hot, add the chicken and fry for 5 minutes, turning regularly, until sealed all over. Add the pepper, spring onions, baby corn, mangetout and red chilli slices. Add a little more oil and fry for 10 minutes, turning the ingredients over regularly.

2   In the meantime, in a small bowl mix together the coconut milk, chilli powder and peanut butter, and season with salt and pepper, to make a sauce.

3   Add the sauce to the pan with the vegetables and fry for 2 minutes, until bubbling.

4   Stir in the straight-to-wok noodles, breaking them apart as you add them. Add the lime juice and the soy sauce, and fry for 3 minutes on a low heat, moving the noodles around the pan until coated and evenly distributed through the veg.

5   Check that the chicken is cooked through, then divide the stir-fry equally between 4 bowls. Sprinkle with some roughly crushed cashew nuts and chopped coriander to serve, if you wish.

tip: Add extra veg like broccoli and shredded cabbage to make this go further, and use the fresh red chilli if you like it hot.

bacon, spinach & cheese gnocchi

Gnocchi are lovely to make, but they are a bit of a faff and create a lot of mess. So sometimes, like pasta, it's nice just to buy them ready made. This dinner takes around 15 minutes to get on the table, perfect for busy nights when you need a bit of comfort food. The result has a strong, rich flavour, so is best served with a crisp salad.

feeds 2 | 15min

olive oil, for frying
2 rashers of smoked bacon, cut into 2cm pieces
2 shallots, finely sliced
500g gnocchi
150g mature spreadable cheese
60ml whole milk
squeeze of lemon juice
50g frozen spinach, defrosted and roughly chopped
green salad, to serve
freshly ground black pepper

1 Drizzle a little oil into a large, non-stick frying pan on a medium heat. When hot, add the bacon and shallots and fry for 5 minutes, until the shallots have softened.

2 Add the gnocchi to the pan and a little more oil. Move the mixture around the pan until the gnocchi are coated in oil and fry them for 5-7 minutes, until heated through and beginning to turn a golden brown.

3 In the meantime, place the spreadable cheese in a bowl with the milk and lemon, and whisk until smooth to make a sauce. Stir in the spinach and season with black pepper.

4 Add the cheese and spinach sauce to the pan. Stir on a low heat until just boiling. Serve with salad.

tip: If you want to make this vegetarian, just swap the bacon for finely sliced mushrooms and ½ teaspoon smoked paprika. All of the smoky flavour without the meat!

chorizo marinara

Everyone needs a really simple pasta recipe in their life – a recipe that turns basic, storecupboard ingredients into a great-tasting meal. This is one of those recipes.

feeds 4 | 20min

olive oil, for frying
1 onion, finely chopped
½ chorizo ring, skin removed, chopped into small pieces
2 garlic cloves, finely chopped
1 tablespoon balsamic vinegar
pinch of mild or hot chilli powder (depending on how spicy you like it)
1 teaspoon dried oregano
2 x 400g tins of chopped tomatoes
400g spaghetti
small handful of flat-leaf parsley, finely chopped, to serve (optional)
salt and freshly ground black pepper

1 Drizzle a little oil into a saucepan on a medium heat. Add the onion and fry for 5 minutes, until softened. Add the chorizo and garlic and fry for 3 minutes, stirring occasionally, until the garlic has softened and the chorizo has released some of its oil. Add the balsamic, chilli powder and oregano. Fry for a further 1 minute, then stir in the tomatoes and season with salt and pepper. Reduce the heat to low and simmer for 10 minutes, stirring occasionally, to allow the flavours to mingle.

2 While the sauce is simmering, cook the pasta. Break the spaghetti in half and place in a saucepan. Cover with boiling water, then salt the water and place on a high heat. Bring to the boil, then reduce the heat and simmer for 10 minutes, or until the pasta is tender.

3 Using tongs or a fork, lift the cooked pasta from the saucepan and place it in the pan of sauce. Move the spaghetti around the pan until coated. Serve in bowls, sprinkled with chopped parsley, if you wish.

tip: You can swap chorizo for bacon lardons if you prefer – or leave out the meat altogether. It will still taste amazing.

steak fajitas

feeds 4 | 20min

olive oil, for frying
400g frying steak, cut
 into bite-sized pieces
1 red pepper, deseeded
 and finely sliced
1 yellow pepper, deseeded
 and finely sliced
1 onion, finely sliced
4 teaspoons beef gravy
 granules
2 teaspoons paprika
1 teaspoon chilli powder
1 teaspoon ground cumin
2 tablespoons tomato
 purée
150ml boiling water
salt and freshly ground
 black pepper

to serve
6 flour tortillas
mayonnaise or soured
 cream (optional)
2 handfuls of shredded
 lettuce
handful of mature
 cheddar cheese, grated
 (optional)
small handful of
 coriander, finely
 chopped, to serve
 (optional)

hob *quick dinners*

Of all the dinners I make, this one is probably the kids' favourite. It is the ultimate happy dinner in our house. Adding gravy granules gives a lovely, saucy beefiness to the fajita mixture that I think sets it apart from chicken fajitas.

1 Drizzle a little oil into a flat-bottomed wok or large frying pan on a medium heat. When hot, add the beef, both peppers and onion and fry for 10 minutes, stirring regularly, until the beef has taken on some colour and the peppers have softened.

2 In the meantime, mix the gravy granules, paprika, chilli powder, cumin and tomato purée in a small bowl and season with salt and pepper. Pour the boiling water over and stir until you have a smooth sauce.

3 Pour the sauce into the pan and simmer for 5 minutes, stirring regularly, until the beef is cooked through and coated in the sauce.

4 To serve, lay out the tortillas. Spread a little mayonnaise or soured cream, if using, on each one, and top with some shredded lettuce.

5 Divide the beef fajita filling equally between the wraps and finish with a little grated cheese, and a sprinkling of coriander, if you wish.

6 To serve, fold over each wrap, or tuck in the sides, roll them up, and cut them in half (serve 3 halves per person).

tip: If you want to make it veggie, try using cook-from-frozen vegetarian beef strips.

lamb & lentil keema flat breads

feeds 4 | 30min

for the flat breads
400g plain flour
1 teaspoon salt
1 teaspoon baking
  powder
400g Greek yoghurt, plus
  a little extra if needed
freshly ground black
  pepper

**for the lamb & lentil
  keema**
olive oil, for frying
1 onion, finely chopped
475g lamb mince
2 garlic cloves, finely
  chopped
1 tablespoon runny honey
1 tablespoon tomato
  purée
1-2 teaspoons chilli
  powder
1 teaspoon ground cumin
1 teaspoon ground
  coriander
1 teaspoon ground
  turmeric
1 tablespoon tomato
  ketchup
1 x 400g tin of green
  lentils, drained
150ml vegetable stock
salt and freshly ground
  black pepper

to serve (optional)
1 red chilli, sliced into
  rings
soured cream
picked coriander leaves

You can buy ready-made flat breads for this recipe if you're short on time, but these are quick to put together and I love making them. I often cook double the quantity of flatbreads and freeze them for quick lunches. Just thoroughly defrost the cooked flatbreads and warm them through in a pan. You can brush them with melted butter and finely chopped garlic before heating them to make a quick garlic bread.

You can use beef mince for the recipe if you prefer, but I think the lamb goes well with the earthy flavours of the lentils.

1 First, make the flat breads. Mix the flour with the salt and baking powder and season with black pepper. Stir in the yoghurt until you have a dough, adding a little more yoghurt if needed. Gently knead the dough on a floured surface until it forms a smooth ball. Divide the dough into 8 equal pieces. Using a rolling pin, roll out each piece to a thick oval, roughly 15-20cm long and ½-1cm thick.

2 Heat a non-stick frying pan or griddle. Fry the flat breads in the dry pan for 2 minutes on each side, until puffy in places and lightly coloured, and set aside while you make the keema.

3 Drizzle a little oil into the same frying pan and place on a medium heat. Add the onion and fry for 5 minutes, until softened.

4 Add the mince and fry for 5 minutes, until browned. Drain off any excess fat. Stir in the garlic, honey, tomato purée, chilli powder, cumin, coriander, turmeric, ketchup and lentils and fry for 1 minute. Season with salt and pepper and stir in the stock. Simmer for 5-10 minutes on a medium heat, until the lamb is cooked through and most of the stock has evaporated but the mixture is still wet.

5 Place 2 flat breads on each plate. Divide the lamb and lentils between the flat breads and serve topped with slices of chilli, spoonfuls of soured cream and a few picked coriander leaves, if you wish.

weekend food

This chapter is where you'll find your food for the weekend. Mouthwatering fakeaways, guilty pleasures and Saturday night treats. These recipes aren't just a joy to eat, they are also a joy to cook.

one-pan pizza

My kids love this recipe because ... well, because it's pizza! I love this recipe because it means I'm able to get a homemade pizza on the table in under 15 minutes! The yeast-free dough is thin and beautifully crisp and the mozzarella and pesto combination is melt-in-the-mouth.

makes 1 pizza | 15min

110g plain flour
1 teaspoon olive oil, plus a little extra for frying
1 tablespoon tomato purée
1 tablespoon tomato ketchup
½ ball of mozzarella
1–2 teaspoons green pesto
pinch of dried oregano
salt and freshly ground black pepper

1 First, make the pizza dough. In a bowl, mix the flour and olive oil together with 50ml water and season with salt and pepper, combining to a dough. Tip out the dough on to a floured work surface and knead for a minute or so, until smooth. Roll out the dough into a circle, roughly 20cm in diameter.

2 Brush a thin layer of oil around the bottom of a non-stick frying pan. Heat the pan on a medium heat and add the dough circle. Fry for 3–4 minutes on a medium heat, until crisp, golden and partially cooked through.

3 In the meantime, prep the topping. Mix the tomato purée and ketchup together. Finely slice the mozzarella using a serrated knife so that you can cut it nice and thinly. Then, halve each slice.

4 Carefully turn the dough over in the pan and take the pan off the heat. Spread the purée mixture right up to the edges of the pizza base. Lay the mozzarella evenly over the top.

5 Drizzle a little pesto around the cheese and finish with a sprinkle of oregano and a grinding of black pepper.

6 Cover the top of the pan with foil, and return it to a medium heat. Fry the pizza for a further 3–4 minutes without taking off the foil (it traps in the heat). If there is a little liquid from the mozzarella sitting on the pizza, just gently tip it, letting it run off into the hot pan. Remove the pizza from the pan and leave to rest for a minute on a chopping board before cutting into slices to serve.

tip: Other toppings to try are ricotta, jarred artichokes, sundried tomatoes, olives, pine nuts or gorgonzola.

veggie one-pan burritos

feeds 4 | 30min

olive oil, for frying
1 onion, finely chopped
1 garlic clove, finely
  chopped
100ml boiling water
2 teaspoons beef gravy
  granules (usually
  vegetarian, but check)
½ teaspoon paprika
½ teaspoon ground
  coriander
2 teaspoons ground
  cumin
1 teaspoon mild or hot
  chilli powder (depending
  on how spicy you like it)
500g passata
large handful of frozen
  sweetcorn
300g cook-from-frozen
  vegetarian mince
1 x 400g tin of kidney
  beans (not drained)
1 x 250g pouch of cooked
  basmati rice
large handful of grated
  mature cheddar cheese
large handful of shredded
  Iceberg lettuce
6 flour tortillas, to serve
soured cream, to serve
  (optional)
salt and freshly ground
  black pepper

This is my all-in-one method of making a burrito – even the lettuce and cheese goes in the pan! Perfect for busy weekends, or midweek dinners when you're on the go.

1   Drizzle a little oil into a large, non-stick frying or sauté pan with a lid, and place on a medium heat. (If you don't have the right pan, use a heavy-bottomed saucepan with a lid.) Add the onion and fry on a medium heat for 5 minutes, until softened. Add the garlic and fry for a further 1 minute to soften.

2   In the meantime, mix the boiling water with the gravy granules in a mug. Stir in the paprika, coriander, cumin and chilli powder, until you have a thick sauce. Pour the sauce over the onions and garlic and cook gently for 1 minute.

3   Stir in the passata, frozen sweetcorn, vegetarian mince and kidney beans (including the water from the tin), season with salt and pepper, and bring to the boil. Simmer on a medium heat for 5 minutes, then add the rice, breaking it up with the back of a wooden spoon as you stir, until all the grains are separated. Reduce the heat and simmer on low for 10 minutes, until the rice is piping hot throughout.

4   Sprinkle the cheese over the top of the sauce, arrange the lettuce over the cheese and turn off the heat. Place the lid on the pan and rest the filling for 3–5 minutes, until the lettuce has wilted a little and the cheese has melted. Divide the filling between the wraps, adding a little dollop of soured cream on each, if you wish.

tip: I like to make this veggie as I find it an easy way to make one of our weekly dinners meat-free, but you could use beef mince, if you prefer.

'roasted' cauliflower mac & cheese

This recipe combines two of my favourite dinners: cauliflower cheese and macaroni cheese. There are pieces of cauliflower mixed in with the macaroni and a bacon crumb topping to add a bit of crunch. The flavour combination is wonderful. I should be recommending that you serve this with salad, but I love it with garlic ciabatta!

feeds 4 | 50min

oil for frying
7 rashers streaky
  smoked bacon
300g cauliflower, cut
  into 3–5cm florets
50g butter
50g plain flour
800ml whole milk
300g macaroni
pinch of mild or hot chilli
  powder (depending on
  how spicy you like it)
100g mature cheddar
  cheese, grated
100g smoked cheddar
  cheese, grated (or use
  all mature cheddar if
  you prefer)
small handful flat-leaf
  parsley, very finely
  chopped, to serve
  (optional)
garlic ciabatta (see page
  106), to serve
salt and freshly ground
  black pepper

1 Drizzle a little oil in a large non-stick saucepan with a lid. Heat to medium-high and add the bacon. Fry the bacon for 5 minutes, turning occasionally, until very crispy, then set aside.

2 Add the cauliflower florets to the hot bacon fat, stir and fry on a medium-high heat for 10 minutes, stirring regularly. It will start to soften and take on a lot of colour. Don't worry if there are any charred bits of cauliflower, it will add to the flavour. Set aside.

3 Turn the heat down to low and add the butter. When the butter has melted, stir in the flour. When bubbling, gradually start adding the milk, a little at a time, stirring continuously. Bring the mixture to the boil each time before adding more milk.

4 When you have added all the milk, stir in 500ml water, the macaroni and chilli powder and season with salt and pepper. Bring the sauce to a gentle boil on a low heat.

5 Place the lid on the pan and place the pan on the smallest burner on the lowest heat setting. Simmer the mixture for 10 minutes, then stir the cauliflower into the sauce and return the lid to the pan. Simmer for a further 10 minutes. Stir the pasta every 5 minutes or so to ensure the pasta isn't sticking to the bottom of the pan.

6 While the pasta is cooking, use a heavy knife to cut the bacon into small pieces, the size of breadcrumbs.

7 When the macaroni is tender and the cauliflower has softened but still has a bit of bite to it, stir in the cheese until melted. You will now have a thick, velvety sauce. Leave to rest for 3 minutes.

8 Tip into a serving bowl and sprinkle with the bacon crumbs, a generous amount of ground black pepper and finely chopped parsley, if you wish. And, of course, garlic bread on the side.

spiced chickpea samosas

Samosas are very satisfying to make, particularly on a lazy Sunday. They look fiddly, but they're easy with the right recipe. This one substitutes chickpeas for the traditional cubed potato – you get a similar consistency, but the mixture cooks down much more quickly. I serve them with a little yoghurt and a salad.

makes 16 | 45min

olive oil, for frying
1 onion, finely chopped
1 x 400g tin of chickpeas, drained
2 carrots, finely chopped
2 handfuls of frozen peas
2 teaspoons garam masala
1 teaspoon ground cumin
1 teaspoon mild or hot chilli powder (depending on how spicy you like it)
1 teaspoon black onion seeds
2 tablespoons tomato purée
200ml vegetable stock
50g butter
16 sheets of filo pastry
sesame seeds, to serve (optional)
small handful of coriander, finely picked, to serve (optional)
salt and freshly ground black pepper

1 Drizzle a little oil into a large, non-stick frying pan on a low heat. Add the onion, chickpeas and carrots and fry for 10 minutes, stirring regularly, until the onions and chickpeas are softened and the carrots have lost their hard edge (don't worry if the carrots aren't quite as soft as you'd like yet). Add the frozen peas and cook for 2 minutes, until heated through.

2 Stir in the garam masala, cumin, chilli powder, black onion seeds and tomato purée. Fry for 2 minutes, then add the vegetable stock, and season with salt and pepper. Simmer on low for 10 minutes, stirring regularly, until the stock has been absorbed and the carrots are tender. Place the mixture in a bowl and set aside to cool.

3 Rinse and dry the frying pan, then add the butter and melt on a low heat. Turn off the heat once the butter is liquid.

4 Lay a sheet of filo pastry on the worktop. Brush both sides with the melted butter from the pan, right up to the edges.

5 Lay the pastry, so that a long side runs left to right in front of you. Fold one third of the long end of the pastry towards the centre and do the same for the other end, overlaying the first fold as if you were folding a business letter, so that you have a triple-layered piece of pastry.

6 With a short edge closest to you, place 1 tablespoon of the mixture a few centimetres in from the bottom of the strip.

7 Hold the bottom left hand corner and carefully lift it diagonally over the mixture, until it joins to the right-hand side of the pastry, giving you a triangle.

8 Press the edges of the pastry together and carefully move the filling around the inside of the triangle so that it goes into all 3 corners.

9 Fold the filled triangle upwards, onto the filo rectangle. Continue folding the triangle upwards until you have used up all the pastry. You should be left with a small flap at the end; fold that over the triangle to seal the final edge. Repeat with the remaining pastry sheets and filling.

10 Add oil to the butter pan so that it covers the bottom, and heat until spitting hot. Fry the samosas on a medium heat for 3–4 minutes on each side, until crisp and golden. Sprinkle with a few sesame seeds and a few coriander leaves and serve.

vegetable katsu curry

feeds 4 | 20min

vegetable oil, for frying
½ aubergine, cut into
   bite-sized pieces
1 red pepper, deseeded
   and cut into bite-sized
   pieces
1 yellow pepper, deseeded
   and cut into bite-sized
   pieces
1 courgette, cut into
   thick slices
bunch of spring onions,
   white and green parts
   roughly chopped
140g baby corn, halved
   lengthways
large handful of
   mangetout
2 x 250g pouches of
   cooked long grain rice
50ml boiling water
1 tablespoon dark
   soy sauce
salt and freshly ground
   black pepper

for the katsu sauce
vegetable oil, for frying
1 onion, finely chopped
2 garlic cloves, finely
   chopped
1 tablespoon runny honey
1 tablespoon dark
   soy sauce
1 tablespoon medium
   curry powder
½ teaspoon ground
   ginger
2 tablespoons plain flour
300ml vegetable stock

This is probably the simplest katsu sauce recipe you'll ever find, and it tastes just like the real thing! I love to use a range of vegetables, but you can just serve the sauce with breaded chicken, salad and rice if you'd prefer.

   This is a great way to use up odd bits of veg, so if you don't have anything on the ingredients list, just chop and change for roughly the equivalent. Sweet potatoes, red onion, sugar snap peas and carrots are all good substitutions.

1   Drizzle a little oil into a flat-bottomed wok on a high heat. Add the aubergine, both peppers, and the courgette, spring onions, baby corn and mangetout and fry for 10 minutes, until softened.

2   In the meantime, make the sauce. Drizzle a little oil into a small, non-stick saucepan on a medium heat. Add the onion and fry for 5 minutes, until softened. Add the garlic, honey, soy sauce, curry powder and ginger. Fry for 2 minutes to cook out the spices, then stir in the flour and fry for a further 1 minute.

3   Gradually add the vegetable stock, a little at a time, bringing it to the boil before you add more. Whisk as you go. When you've added all the stock, blitz with a hand blender until smooth.

4   Simmer the sauce on a high heat for 3-5 minutes, until it has reduced and thickened. Remember it will thicken more as it cools. Season with salt and pepper and pour the sauce into a jug. Leave to cool for a few minutes.

5   Add the rice, boiling water and soy sauce to the fried veg, and season with salt and pepper. Fry for 5-7 minutes on a medium-high heat, breaking the rice up as you stir, until heated through.

6   When the rice mixture is fully heated through, divide it between 4 bowls and serve. Leave the sauce in the centre of the table so that everyone can help themselves.

szechuan spaghetti

This is a great alternative to a takeaway. An easy, filling, delicious dinner, it can be on the table in under 30 minutes. The finished dish packs quite a lot of heat, so reduce the quantity of crushed peppercorns you use if you don't like your food too spicy.

feeds 4 | 25min

olive oil, for frying
½ small head of broccoli,
  broken into florets
½ small head of
  cauliflower, broken
  into florets
1 onion, finely sliced
500g turkey mince
2 garlic cloves, finely
  chopped
thumb-sized piece of
  fresh ginger, peeled and
  finely chopped
2 tablespoons dark
  soy sauce
1 teaspoon crushed
  peppercorns
pinch of hot chilli powder
2 tablespoons smooth
  peanut butter
300ml chicken stock
350g dried spaghetti
1 red chilli, finely sliced
  into rings, to serve
  (optional)
small handful of
  coriander, finely
  chopped, to serve
  (optional)
salt

1   Drizzle a little oil into a large saucepan on a medium heat. Add the broccoli, cauliflower and onion and fry for 7 minutes, stirring regularly, until the vegetables have softened a little.

2   Add the turkey mince to the pan, using a spatula to break it up, and fry for 5 minutes, until browned. In the meantime, boil a kettle for the pasta.

3   Mix the garlic, ginger, soy sauce, peppercorns, chilli powder and peanut butter together in a small bowl. Add to the pan and fry for 2 minutes. Next add the stock and gently simmer on a medium-low heat for 10 minutes, stirring regularly.

4   In the meantime, place the spaghetti in a separate saucepan and cover with boiling water. Salt the water, place over a high heat, bring to the boil, then reduce the heat and simmer for 10 minutes, until tender.

5   When the spaghetti is cooked, use tongs or forks to lift the pasta from the pan and place it in the mince and vegetable sauce. Toss the spaghetti around until coated and the ingredients are evenly distributed. Serve immediately, sprinkled with fresh chilli and coriander if you wish.

tip: You can swap the turkey mince for beef or pork, if you prefer.

popcorn chicken nachos

This is a fun, weekend, eat-in-front-of-a-film kind of dinner. If you don't want to serve it on nachos, just make the chicken strips and serve them with salad. And if you're worried about the amount of Cajun spice, don't be. A lot of the heat is lost in cooking, making it warm rather than hot.

feeds 4 | 30min

150g cornflakes
3 teaspoons Cajun spice
1 teaspoon salt
3 eggs, beaten
2 handfuls of plain flour
600g mini chicken fillets;
  or chicken strips, cut into
  2–3cm pieces
olive oil, for frying
180g tortilla chips
2 handfuls grated mature
  cheddar cheese
freshly ground black
  pepper

to finish
8 baby or cherry
  tomatoes, roughly
  chopped
jalapeño slices from a jar
  (roughly 10–15)
soured cream
picked coriander leaves
  (optional)
salad leaves, to serve

1 Place the cornflakes in a bowl. Use your hands to scrunch them up into small pieces. This will take a couple of minutes. Don't be tempted to use a food processor as the pieces will be too fine. Stir in the Cajun spice and salt, and season with pepper.

2 Place the beaten eggs and flour each into a separate bowl.

3 Take a handful of chicken pieces and toss them in the flour until coated. Then, dip each piece of chicken in the egg, shaking off any excess. Roll the chicken in the cornflake crumb until coated and set aside. Repeat for all the remaining chicken.

4 Cover the bottom of a large, non-stick frying pan in oil. Heat over a high heat until spitting, then reduce the heat to medium.

5 In batches, if necessary, add the coated chicken to the pan, frying for 5–7 minutes, or until the chicken is cooked through. Turn the pieces over regularly and adjust the heat if they're cooking too fast. When all the chicken is cooked, set it aside. Rinse and dry the frying pan.

6 Arrange half the tortilla chips so they cover the bottom of the frying pan. Sprinkle with a handful of cheese. Arrange the remaining tortilla chips over the cheese, to create another layer. Finish with another handful of cheese.

7 Turn the heat to its lowest setting and place the pan on top. Heat the tortilla chips for about 5 minutes, gently shaking the pan every so often, until the chips are toasted and the cheese is melted.

8 In the meantime, arrange the popcorn chicken over the top of the tortillas and finish with the chopped tomatoes, sliced jalapeños and spoonfuls of soured cream. Sprinkle with coriander, if you wish, and serve with salad.

'nduja burgers with chipotle 'mayo'

If you've not tried cooking with 'nduja yet, this recipe will be the beginning of something! It's a vivid red, spicy salami paste that packs a huge punch of flavour. Be warned, the mayo is hot, but it goes perfectly with the rich flavour of the burger. You'll need to make the 'mayo' a few hours before you intend to serve.

feeds 4 | 35min

olive oil, for frying
150g shallots, finely sliced
3 tablespoons 'nduja
  paste
handful of coriander,
  finely chopped
500g lean beef mince
4 cheese slices (I use
  gouda)
4 brioche burger buns
salt and freshly ground
  black pepper

for the chipotle 'mayo'
120g soured cream
1 teaspoon chipotle
  chilli powder
small handful of
  coriander, finely
  chopped
pinch of ground cumin
½ teaspoon runny honey
squeeze of lemon juice

to serve (optional)
4 lettuce leaves
small handful of cherry
  tomatoes, sliced
a few jalapeño slices
  from a jar

1 A couple of hours before you intend to serve, place all the 'mayo' ingredients in a small bowl. Stir until smooth and combined. Cover the bowl and refrigerate the mayo until you need it.

2 Make the burgers. Drizzle a little oil into a large, non-stick frying pan on a medium heat. Add the shallots and fry for 10 minutes, until well softened. Stir in the 'nduja paste and the coriander, then season with salt and pepper. Set aside to cool.

3 Place the beef mince in a large bowl and pour over the cooled shallot and 'nduja mixture. Don't worry about washing the pan, as you'll need it to fry the burgers. Use your hands to mix the ingredients together until the beef is red from the paste and the shallots and coriander are evenly distributed.

4 Divide the beef into 4 equal-sized balls. Shape them into burgers, pressing the beef together, ensuring that they are the same thickness all way through, right up to the edges. This will help them to hold their shape in the pan and ensure they cook evenly.

5 Heat a little more oil in the pan until hot. Add the burgers and fry on a medium heat for 4 minutes each side, or until cooked through, placing a slice of cheese on each burger for the last minute of cooking, allowing it to melt over the top.

6 Remove the burgers from the pan, setting aside on a plate to rest for 3 minutes.

7 Slice open the brioche buns. To serve, place a lettuce leaf on the bottom half of each bun and top with the cheesy burgers, then a few slices of tomato and jalapeño if you wish. Spread the cut side of the bun lid with a generous amount of chipotle mayo. Put the lid on the burger and serve immediately.

philly cheesesteak

I'm not going to pretend that this is the healthiest dinner in the world, but it is a dinner guaranteed to make everyone happy! If you have leftovers, just pop them in the fridge to have in a toastie the next day.

makes 6 rolls | 20min

olive oil, for frying
1 red pepper, deseeded
  and diced
1 yellow pepper, deseeded
  and diced
1 onion, finely sliced
500g beef skirt or frying
  steak
½ teaspoon freshly
  ground black pepper
½ teaspoon crushed
  sea salt
3–4 slices of gouda or
  mature cheddar cheese
6 brioche hotdog rolls

to serve (optional)
tomato ketchup
American-style mustard
small handful of curly leaf
  parsley, finely chopped,
  to serve (optional)

1 Drizzle a little oil into a large non-stick frying pan on a medium heat. Add both peppers and the onion, and fry for 7 minutes, until the vegetables have softened.

2 In the meantime, use a serrated knife to cut the steak into very thin wafer slices – cut in the same direction as the grain of the meat to make this easier.

3 Add the steak to the pan with the black pepper and sea salt. Turn the heat up a little and fry for 5 minutes, turning regularly, until the beef is cooked.

4 Turn off the heat and lay the cheese slices over the beef and pepper mixture. Leave for 2–3 minutes to allow the beef to rest and the cheese to melt.

5 Using tongs, divide the filling equally between the hotdog rolls, then serve with ketchup, mustard and a sprinkling of parsley, if you wish.

tip: You can use ordinary cheddar, but gouda has a lovely stringy gooeyness to it and it melts quickly over the beef.

salt & pepper pork with couscous

feeds 4 | 20min

for the couscous

220g couscous
olive oil, for frying
½ red pepper, deseeded
  and diced
1 x 400g tin of chickpeas,
  drained
5 spring onions, white
  and green parts cut
  into 2cm pieces
1 teaspoon Cajun spice
1 teaspoon ground
  turmeric
1 teaspoon ground cumin
1 teaspoon mild or hot
  chilli powder (depending
  on how spicy you like it)
1 tablespoon runny honey
250ml boiling water
small handful of
  coriander, finely
  chopped
cucumber slices or
  shredded lettuce,
  to serve
salt and freshly ground
  black pepper

for the pork

4 pork loin steaks
1 teaspoon sea salt
2 teaspoons freshly
  ground black pepper
2 tablespoons plain flour

This is one of my favourite Friday night dinners. It tastes incredible, just as good as any takeaway I've had, but it takes just 20 minutes to get on the table. If you're not a fan of pork, use beef sirloin steaks. The couscous is a great lunch recipe, too; or serve it with barbecued chicken or fish.

1 First, make the couscous. Place the couscous in a large mixing bowl and season with salt and pepper. Set aside.

2 Drizzle a little oil into a large, non-stick frying pan on a medium heat. Add the red pepper, chickpeas and spring onions and fry for 3 minutes, stirring regularly, until the pepper has softened.

3 Stir in the Cajun spice, turmeric, cumin, chilli powder, honey and salt and pepper. Fry for a further 2 minutes, then add the mixture to the couscous and stir until evenly distributed. Set aside the frying pan - you'll need it for the pork.

4 Pour the boiling water over the couscous. Stir once, then cover the bowl with a plate or cling film to trap in the steam. Leave for 10 minutes, removing the covering to stir once half way through, then covering again.

5 Meanwhile, prepare the pork. Use a sharp, serrated knife to cut the pork widthways into thin slices. Put the slices in a bowl.

6 Place the salt and pepper in a pestle and mortar. Grind until fine, then combine with the flour. Sprinkle the seasoned flour over the pork slices, a little at a time, using your hands to ensure all the pieces are thoroughly coated.

7 Heat a glug of oil in the frying pan on a medium-high heat. When hot, add the pork and fry for 5-7 minutes, turning regularly, until the pork is browned and cooked through.

8 Stir the coriander into the couscous and divide equally between 4 bowls. Top with the pork and serve with sliced cucumber, the Jerk Sweet Potato on page 210, or shredded lettuce.

pork, roquefort sauce & colcannon

In my opinion, this is the best way to cook pork so that it's still lovely and juicy. You can make the colcannon ahead of time and reheat it in a saucepan on a low heat. Just add a little more milk to loosen it. The sauce is very rich and has a strong flavour, so use sparingly. Serve with the Steamed Spinach & Cashews on page 214.

feeds 4 | 45min

for the colcannon
40g butter
2 onions, finely sliced
150g savoy cabbage, shredded
1kg potatoes (choose good mashers), peeled and cut into 3–4cm pieces
70ml whole milk
small handful of flat-leaf parsley, leaves picked, to serve (optional)
salt and freshly ground black pepper

for the pork and sauce
4 pork loin steaks
olive oil, for frying
20ml whole milk
85g crème fraîche
150g roquefort cheese, crumbled
salt and freshly ground black pepper

1 First make the colcannon. Place a large saucepan with a lid on a medium heat. Add the butter and allow to melt. Add the onions and cabbage and fry (without the lid) on a medium heat for 10 minutes, stirring regularly, until softened. Scoop out the cabbage and onion mixture, and set aside. Rinse out the pan.

2 Place the potatoes in the pan. Cover them in water, then salt the water and bring it to the boil on a high heat. Reduce the heat and simmer until soft enough to mash. Drain the potatoes and let them steam off in a colander for a couple of minutes. Tip them back into the pan and mash until smooth. Stir in the milk and the onion and cabbage mixture, and season with salt and pepper. If you're eating straightaway, place the lid on the saucepan and the mash will stay hot as you cook the pork and sauce.

3 Season the pork steaks with salt and ground black pepper, rubbing the seasoning into both sides. Heat a glug of oil in a large, non-stick frying pan. When the oil is spitting hot, add the steaks to the pan. Fry on a high heat for 2–3 minutes each side, or until cooked through (thicker steaks may need a little longer).

4 Remove the pork from the pan, setting them aside to rest on a warm plate. Drizzle any fat from the pan over the top.

5 Place the milk, crème fraîche and roquefort in the pork pan (don't worry if there's still a little fat at the bottom). Gently warm on a low heat, stirring continuously, until the cheese has melted and the sauce is smooth. Don't let it boil. Season with pepper.

6 Spoon the colcannon into 4 serving bowls. Top each portion with a pork steak and drizzle with the sauce. Serve sprinkled with parsley, if you wish, and a final grinding of black pepper.

budget wonders

This chapter makes the most of simple, storecupboard ingredients. There are exciting ways to use up leftovers, easy tricks with cheap tins and flavour-filled dinners that use only a handful of ingredients.

veggie sausage, lentil & tomato stew

This is such a satisfying dinner. The consistency is somewhere between a stew and a soup and thick enough to placate even the hungriest members of the family! Serve it with buttered crusty bread.

feeds 4 | 40min

olive oil, for frying
8 vegetarian sausages
   (use a brand you
   can fry)
1 onion, finely chopped
1 red pepper, deseeded
   and finely chopped
½–1 teaspoon chilli flakes
2 garlic cloves, finely
   chopped
1 x 400g tin of chopped
   tomatoes
125g dried red lentils
600ml vegetable stock
small handful of flat-leaf
   parsley, finely chopped,
   to serve (optional)
slices of buttered
   crusty bread, to serve
   (optional)
salt and freshly ground
   black pepper

1 Drizzle a little oil into a large saucepan with a lid, and place on a low heat. Add the sausages and fry (without the lid) for 7-10 minutes, regularly moving them around the pan.

2 Remove the sausages from the pan and add the onion, pepper and a little more oil if necessary. Fry for 5-7 minutes, until the vegetables have softened.

3 Meanwhile, cut each sausage into 4 or 5 pieces, then return the pieces to the pan once the vegetables are soft.

4 Add the chilli flakes and garlic and fry for 1 minute, then pour in the tomatoes. Stir in the lentils and stock, and season with salt and pepper.

5 Bring the stew to the boil, place the lid on the pan and simmer on low for 20 minutes, stirring occasionally, until the lentils are tender. Sprinkle with flat-leaf parsley and serve with slices of buttered crusty bread, if you wish.

tip: You can use meat sausages if you prefer, just make sure they're cooked through as they may need a little longer.

margherita strata

This is basically a next-level omelette! It is a life saver when the cupboards are looking a bit bare and you're short on time. Pack out the egg with more veggies if you have them – asparagus, peppers and courgette all work well. Just add them to the pan with the tomatoes. Serve with lettuce and cucumber, or with the Warm Bean Salad on page 215.

feeds 2 | 25min

olive oil, for frying
2 slices of bread, cut into 3cm cubes
10 firm cherry or baby tomatoes, halved
5 eggs
60g cheddar cheese, grated
1 heaped teaspoon green pesto
shredded lettuce and sliced cucumber, to serve (optional)
salt and freshly ground black pepper

1   Pour a glug of oil into a large saucepan with a lid and place on a medium heat. The pan should be roughly 25-28cm across with a good, non-stick bottom. Add the bread pieces and fry, turning regularly, for 3-5 minutes, until the bread is golden brown and toasted. Set the bread aside and add the tomatoes to the pan with a little more oil. Fry for 3-5 minutes, until beginning to soften.

2   In the meantime, beat the eggs together in a bowl and stir in the grated cheese and pesto. Season with salt and pepper.

3   Turn the heat to its lowest setting on the smallest burner. Return the bread to the pan and pour the egg over the tomatoes and bread, ensuring they are evenly spread before the egg sets. Place the lid on the pan and cook for 10-15 minutes, or until the egg on top is just set.

4   Sprinkle with a little extra black pepper, cut the strata into wedges, and serve with salad.

tip: You can use fresh basil leaves if you prefer, but pesto is an easy, cheap way to add great flavour.

feta ratatouille & garlic ciabatta

Leftover veg simply loves a ratatouille. If you don't have everything I've suggested, feel free to substitute some of the ingredients for whatever you do have in your vegetable drawer. Use extra courgette if you don't have aubergine, for example; or chopped tinned tomatoes, if you haven't got fresh. You don't have to use feta, but it does give a lovely, salty flavour. And, as a bonus, this is the meal that keeps on giving – add a little water to any leftovers and blitz with a hand blender to make a quick pasta sauce.

feeds 4 | 40min

olive oil, for frying
1 courgette, cut into
  2cm cubes
½ aubergine, cut into
  2cm cubes
1 onion, roughly chopped
1 red pepper, deseeded
  and cut into 3cm pieces
1 yellow pepper, deseeded
  and cut into 3cm pieces
7 cherry tomatoes, halved
2 garlic cloves, finely
  chopped
1 teaspoon light brown
  soft sugar
1 tablespoon balsamic
  vinegar
1 teaspoon dried oregano
500g passata
150g feta cheese,
  crumbled
small handful of flat-leaf
  parsley, finely chopped,
  to serve (optional)

1   Add a good glug of oil to a large saucepan with a lid, and place on a medium-high heat. Add the courgette, aubergine, onion and both peppers and fry (without the lid) for 10 minutes, stirring regularly, until the vegetables have a little colour and are beginning to soften.

2   Add the tomatoes and garlic. Turn the heat to medium and fry for a further 5 minutes, until the garlic is soft and the tomatoes have broken down a little. Stir in the sugar, balsamic vinegar and oregano. Fry for 2 minutes, then stir in the passata. Reduce the heat to low and simmer for 15 minutes, stirring occasionally, until you have a thick, rich stew.

3   In the meantime, make the garlic ciabatta. Melt the butter in a non-stick frying pan on a low heat.

4   Peel the garlic cloves and carefully crush them with a rolling pin, so that they're mostly still intact.

5   Add the garlic to the butter and fry gently for 1-2 minutes, then remove the cloves from the pan and discard. Decant half the melted butter from the pan and set aside.

6   Add 4 of the ciabatta bottoms to the pan, turning them over until they're coated in butter. Fry for 2-3 minutes on each side, pressing down gently with a spatula, until they're crisp and golden. Season with pepper, remove from the pan and set aside on a plate. Return the remaining butter to the pan and repeat the process with the ciabatta tops.

for the garlic ciabatta
50g butter
2 garlic cloves
4 ciabatta rolls, halved
freshly ground black
*   pepper*

7 Sprinkle the crumbled feta over the cooked ratatouille, place the lid on the pan and turn off the heat. Leave for 5 minutes to allow the feta to melt a little (or you can sprinkle on the feta as you serve, if you prefer).

8 To serve, place a garlic ciabatta top and bottom into each serving bowl. Spoon over the ratatouille and sprinkle with a little flat-leaf parsley, if you wish.

butternut saag

This is my take on a saag aloo, swapping the potato for butternut squash. It's quick, simple and tastes the same as a takeaway! To make it a quick dinner, you need to cut the butternut squash into small pieces. The recipe uses frozen spinach, but you can use fresh – just don't add it until 5 minutes before the end of cooking. Serve with rice.

feeds 2–4 | 30min

olive oil, for frying
1 large butternut squash, cut into 1-2cm cubes
1 onion, finely sliced
2 garlic cloves, finely chopped
1 teaspoon ground turmeric
1 teaspoon black onion seeds
½ teaspoon ground ginger
1 teaspoon mild or hot chilli powder (depending on how spicy you like it)
1 teaspoon ground cumin
2 tablespoons tomato purée
150g frozen spinach, defrosted and roughly chopped
300ml vegetable stock
cooked rice and naan breads, to serve
salt and freshly ground black pepper

1 Drizzle a little oil into a large, non-stick saucepan with a lid, and place on a medium heat. Add the butternut squash and fry (without the lid), turning the squash over occasionally, for 10-15 minutes, or until tender.

2 Add the onion and a little more oil. Fry for a further 5 minutes, stirring regularly, until the onion is softened, then stir in the garlic, turmeric, black onion seeds, ginger, chilli powder, cumin and tomato purée. Fry for 1 minute, then add the spinach and the stock, and season with salt and pepper.

3 Place the lid on the pan and simmer the mixture on a low heat for 5 minutes, then take the lid off the pan, increase the heat a little and simmer for a further 5 minutes, until the squash is cooked and the sauce has reduced. Serve with rice and naan breads.

tip: If you want to make an even quicker version of this, just swap the squash for two tins of drained potatoes. Cut them in half and add to the pan with the onion. It will cook in half the time.

spicy bean burgers

These spicy bean burgers have such a satisfying texture and delicious flavour – they are sure to appeal to even the most dedicated meat-eater. They are much more filling than regular burgers, so you won't need to serve them with anything except a bun, a side salad and maybe a slice of cheese.

makes 6 | 30min

2 x 400g tins of mixed beans in water, drained
100g fresh breadcrumbs
1 carrot, roughly grated
80g drained tinned sweetcorn
80g spicy cheddar cheese, roughly grated (or use mature cheddar)
2 spring onions, very finely chopped
1 teaspoon hot chilli powder
1 teaspoon ground cumin
1 teaspoon ground coriander
1 teaspoon runny honey
handful of plain flour
olive oil, for frying
6 burger buns
salt and freshly ground black pepper

to serve (optional)

lettuce leaves and cucumber slices, or a side salad
mayonnaise
slices of your favourite cheese

1. Place the drained beans in a large mixing bowl. Mash them with the end of a rolling pin or the pestle from a pestle and mortar. Finish off by mashing them with a fork – it doesn't have to be completely lump free, as long as most of it is (some of the beans can just be broken up).

2. Stir in the breadcrumbs, carrot, sweetcorn, cheddar, spring onions, chilli powder, cumin, ground coriander and honey, and season with salt and pepper.

3. Work the ingredients through the beans with your hands to ensure that everything is thoroughly combined.

4. Divide the mixture into 6 balls, pressing them together firmly in your hands. Sprinkle the flour over a plate and roll each of the balls in the flour until they have a light coating. Press the balls into burger shapes, making sure they are the same thickness all the way through.

5. Heat a couple of glugs of oil in a large, non-stick frying pan on a medium-high heat. When the oil is hot, in batches, fry the burgers for 5 minutes on each side (don't move them for at least 4 minutes, as this will help them to stay together in the pan). Set each batch aside on a plate while you fry the remainder – it's good to allow them to cool a little before serving, as this will make them firmer.

6. Place each burger in a bun and serve topped with lettuce and cucumber slices, mayo and slices of cheese, if you wish. Or a side salad is good, too.

tuna spaghetti melt

This is a kid-friendly, easy midweek win. It makes the best of simple storecupboard ingredients, it's on the table in under 30 minutes and it uses only one pan. Add fresh spinach at the end to up the veg content, if you wish.

feeds 4 | 30min

olive oil, for frying
1 onion, finely chopped
2 garlic cloves, finely
    chopped
1 x 400g tin of chopped
    tomatoes
500g passata
950ml litres vegetable
    stock
375g dried spaghetti
2 x 160g tins of tuna
    chunks in spring water,
    drained
150g mature cheddar
    cheese, grated
small handful of basil,
    leaves picked and finely
    chopped
1 ball of mozzarella, thinly
    sliced, or a handful of
    grated mozzarella
small handful of flat-leaf
    parsley, finely chopped,
    to serve
salt and freshly ground
    black pepper

1 Drizzle a little oil into a large saucepan with a lid, and place on a medium heat. Add the onion and fry for 5 minutes, until softened. Add the garlic for the final 1 minute to soften that too.

2 Stir in the tinned tomatoes, passata and stock, and season with salt and pepper. Bring to the boil.

3 Break the spaghetti in half and add it to the pan. Bring the liquid back to the boil and use a fork to carefully separate the spaghetti to ensure that it doesn't stick.

4 Stir, then place the lid on the pan and simmer on a medium heat for 10 minutes, stirring once half way through cooking. Remove the lid and simmer for a further 2 minutes. The sauce will thicken a little and the spaghetti will be tender.

5 Flake the tuna into the pan, then stir in the cheddar and the basil.

6 Arrange the sliced or grated mozzarella over the top. Place the lid on the pan and turn off the heat. Leave to rest for 5 minutes, so that the sauce thickens and the mozzarella melts.

7 Finish with the parsley and a little black pepper, and serve.

tip: If you don't have fresh basil, just stir in a tablespoon of pesto with the tuna.

cheat's kedgeree

This is a simple version of a classic dish using cheap storecupboard ingredients. The spices are mild, so if you like a bit more heat, just add a little chilli or use hot curry powder.

feeds 2 | 15min

2 eggs
1 onion, finely sliced
2 x 160g tins of mackerel in oil
1 tablespoon mild or hot curry powder (depending on how spicy you like it)
2 x 250g pouches of cooked long grain rice
50ml whole milk
small handful of flat-leaf parsley, finely chopped, to serve (optional)
salt and freshly ground black pepper

1   Bring a saucepan of water to a vigorous boil. Gently lower the eggs into the pan with a slotted spoon and simmer for 8 minutes – this will be enough to hard-boil them.

2   While the eggs are cooking, prepare the rice. Place the onion and a drizzle of oil from the mackerel tin in a large, non-stick frying pan. Fry the onion for 5 minutes, stirring occasionally, until softened.

3   Add the curry powder and fry for 1 minute, then add the pouches of rice, the mackerel and the milk. Reduce the heat to low and fry gently for 5 minutes, stirring with a wooden spoon to break up the rice and mackerel. The rice will separate easily as it heats up.

4   When the eggs are ready, place them in a bowl of cold water.

5   When the rice is fully heated through, season with salt and pepper. Divide the kedgeree between 2 plates. Shell the eggs, and cut each egg into quarters. Arrange the quarters over the rice in each bowl. Finish with some finely chopped parsley and a little black pepper before serving, if you wish.

tip: As well as a comforting dinner, kedgeree makes a lovely lunch as you can eat it hot or cold. Just prep it the night before and store it in an airtight container.

easy salmon fishcakes

This is an easy meal using tinned fish and leftover mash. You can use fresh herbs if you prefer, but squeezy herbs from a tube are a handy storecupboard standby and they last a lot longer. If you're not a fan of tinned salmon, use tuna. I love serving this with the Spiced Rice on page 212.

makes 8 | 20min

2 x 213g tins of skinless,
  boneless salmon,
  drained
2 tablespoons
  mayonnaise
2 teaspoons mixed herbs
  from a tube
4 spring onions, green
  and white parts finely
  chopped
700g leftover mashed
  potato
2-3 slices of bread,
  blitzed in a food
  processor to
  breadcrumbs
olive oil, for frying
carrot and cucumber
  salad, to serve
tartare sauce, to serve
salt and freshly ground
  black pepper

1   Place the drained salmon in a mixing bowl and mash it with a fork. Stir in the mayonnaise, herbs and spring onions. Add the mashed potato, and season with salt and pepper, then combine the ingredients until they're evenly distributed. Use your hands as this will help to warm and loosen the cold mashed potato.

2   Divide the mixture into 8 balls. Scatter the breadcrumbs over a plate and roll each ball in the breadcrumbs, before firmly pressing them into fishcakes.

3   Pour a couple of glugs of oil into a large, non-stick frying pan. In batches, if necessary, fry the fishcakes on a medium heat for 3-4 minutes on each side. When they first go in the pan, leave them for a least 3 minutes - don't be tempted to move them around (leaving them will create a crispy shell that will make sure they stay together in the pan). Keep each batch warm while you cook the remainder.

4   Serve with a side salad (I like ribbons of carrot and cucumber) and tartare sauce.

tip: If you don't have any leftover mash, you'll need roughly 4 medium baking potatoes, peeled, boiled and mashed with just a little butter, salt and pepper.

red pesto koftas

I love making these. You can use traditional lamb mince if you prefer, but turkey is cheaper and healthier. I like to have the koftas on flat breads with salad and the feta dressing, but pitta, sautéed veg, rice and hummus work well too. Eat them cold and create your own Buddha bowl – perfect for lunchboxes!

feeds 4 | 25min

500g turkey mince
2 tablespoons red pesto
handful of curly leaf
  parsley, finely chopped,
  plus optional extra
  to serve
3 spring onions, finely
  chopped
olive oil, for frying
salt and freshly ground
  black pepper

for the feta dressing
80g feta
4 heaped dessertspoons
  of full-fat Greek yoghurt
squeeze of lemon juice
freshly ground black
  pepper

to serve
flat breads
cherry tomatoes, halved
red or yellow pepper,
  deseeded and cut
  into strips

1 Add the turkey mince, red pesto, parsley, spring onions and salt and pepper to a large mixing bowl. Use your hands to ensure the ingredients are fully and evenly combined.

2 Divide the mixture into 12-14 balls, pressing them firmly between your hands so you have small, long, oval shapes. Flatten them a little so that they're easier to fry.

3 Drizzle a small amount of oil into a non-stick frying pan on a medium heat. When hot, add the koftas and fry, turning regularly, for about 8-10 minutes, or until cooked through. (Cooking time will vary, depending on the size and thickness of your koftas. When you think the koftas are done, cut the largest in half and check that it's cooked through.)

4 In the meantime, make the feta dressing. Place the feta, yoghurt and lemon juice in a bowl. Using a hand blender, blend until smooth, then stir in a generous amount of black pepper to season. Set aside. (You can make this ahead of time, in which case refrigerate until you're ready to serve.)

5 Serve the kofta on the flat breads with spoonfuls of the dressing. Sprinkle with extra parsley, if you wish, and serve some cherry tomatoes and pepper strips alongside.

french onion chicken

This is one of those 'grab-the-ingredients-on-the-way-home' kind of dinners. It's simple, tasty and smells incredible when it's cooking. Serve it with buttered bread or mashed potato. If you're not a fan of French onion, experiment with different soup flavours.

feeds 4 | 30min

600g skinless, boneless
  chicken thighs
handful of plain flour
olive oil, for frying
large handful of pre-
  shredded kale (discard
  any tough stems)
1 teaspoon dried thyme
1 x 600ml tub of French
  onion soup
1 x 400g tin of cannellini
  beans, drained
buttered bread or
  mashed potato, to serve
salt and freshly ground
  black pepper

1   Open up the chicken thighs and cut them in half. Sprinkle the flour over a plate and roll the fillets in the flour until they have a light dusting.

2   Drizzle a little oil into a large, non-stick saucepan with a lid, and place on a high heat. When hot, add the chicken and fry (without the lid) for 3 minutes on each side, until you start to see a bit of colour developing. Add the kale, thyme and a little more oil and fry for a further 2 minutes to soften the kale a little. Stir in the soup and beans, and season with salt and pepper.

3   Place the lid on the pan and simmer on a low heat for 10-15 minutes, stirring occasionally, until the chicken is cooked through – check the largest piece of chicken in the pan before you serve.

4   Serve with slices of buttered bread or mashed potato.

tip: If you're not a fan of French onion soup, experiment with different soup flavours. Good quality vegetable, mushroom, tomato and lentil or minestrone soup would all work well. Or try any leftover homemade soup! If it's very thick, just water it down a little.

leftover roast chicken & stuffing soup

This is a lovely, thick comforting soup that uses leftover roast ingredients. If you don't mind a soup with a thinner base, add more stock to make it go further.

feeds 2–3 | 20min

40g butter
1 large carrot, peeled and sliced into ribbons
100g savoy cabbage, shredded
1 teaspoon dried mixed herbs
1 teaspoon dark soy sauce
600ml chicken stock
300ml whole milk
200g leftover roast chicken, shredded
4 balls of cooked sage-and-onion stuffing, each one torn into 4 or 5 pieces
salt and freshly ground black pepper

1 Place a saucepan with a lid on a medium heat. Add the butter and (without the lid) allow to melt. Add the carrot and cabbage and fry, stirring regularly, for 5 minutes, until the vegetables are just starting to soften. Add the mixed herbs and soy sauce and fry for 1 minute, then stir in the stock, milk, chicken and stuffing, and season with salt and pepper.

2 Bring to the boil, place the lid on the pan and simmer for 10 minutes, until the chicken is heated through. Sprinkle with extra grindings of black pepper to serve, if you wish.

tip: If you have some leftover roast potatoes, cut them up and throw them in for a truly magnificent dinner.

sausage & apple bubble & squeak cakes

Bubble and squeak is the ultimate budget dinner. These cakes make a filling main, side dish or even brunch. Serve with salad, although I love to have it with baked beans. If you're serving it as brunch, why not try adding a fried egg on top!

feeds 4 | 30min

6-8 pork sausages
olive oil, for frying
1 large onion, finely sliced
200g white or
  sweetheart cabbage,
  finely shredded
650g leftover mashed
  potato
2 eating apples, cored
  and roughly grated
small handful of flour
small handful of curly leaf
  parsley, finely chopped,
  to serve (optional)
salt and freshly ground
  black pepper

1   Use a knife to slit the skins of the sausages. Pull out the meat and discard the skins. Tear the sausage meat into 8 smaller pieces.

2   Drizzle a little oil into a non-stick frying pan on a medium-low heat. When hot, add the sausage pieces, along with the onion and cabbage, and fry for 7-10 minutes, stirring regularly, until the vegetables are soft and the sausage is browned and cooked through.

3   Transfer the mixture to a mixing bowl with the leftover mashed potato and grated apple, and season with salt and pepper. Use your hands to combine all the ingredients, as this will help to warm and loosen the cold mashed potato.

4   Divide the mixture into 8 patties, roughly 8-9cm wide and 2cm deep. Sprinkle a little flour onto the worktop and turn each of the cakes over in the flour until coated.

5   Heat a little more oil in the pan on a medium-high heat. When the oil is hot, fry the potato cakes in batches on a medium-high heat for around 5 minutes, until the bottom is crisp and brown. Carefully turn the cakes over and fry for another 4-5 minutes until crisp and heated through.

6   Sprinkle with parsley, if using, and finish with an extra grinding of black pepper, before serving.

tip: If you're making the bubble and squeak from scratch, rather than using leftovers, you'll need to peel, boil and mash about 4 medium baking potatoes first.

a low simmer

The recipes in this chapter require a bit more time and a bit more care – they are labour-of-love cooking and worth every minute. Think slow-cooked meat that melts in the mouth, hearty stews and creamy risottos. These are full-bodied dinners that are just what you need if you're after a bit of comfort.

creamy harissa penne

This pasta sauce packs in a lot of flavour and heat – vary the number of chillies you use, depending on who you're making it for. Or, pierce the chillies several times and add them whole, then remove them before serving – you'll get warmth without the sauce becoming too hot.

feeds 4 | 40min

2 large red peppers, deseeded and cut into 3cm pieces/cubes
2–3 red chillies, cut in half lengthways and deseeded
3 garlic cloves, peeled and halved
2 tablespoons olive oil
375g penne pasta
1 teaspoon smoked paprika
½ teaspoon ground cumin
1 teaspoon ground coriander
1 teaspoon runny honey
1 tablespoon tomato purée
50ml whole milk
salt and freshly ground black pepper

1   Place the peppers, chillies, garlic cloves and oil in a large non-stick saucepan with a lid. Place the lid on the pan and gently fry on a low heat for 30 minutes, removing the lid from time to time to stir, until the vegetables are cooked.

2   In the meantime, 10 minutes before the end of the cooking time, place the pasta in a separate saucepan and cover in boiling water. Salt the water and bring to the boil, then simmer for 10 minutes, until tender.

3   Remove the lid from the peppers and chilli mixture and stir in the paprika, cumin, ground coriander, honey and tomato purée. Fry for 2 minutes, still on a low heat, then add the milk, season with salt and pepper, and stir to gather any spices that may have stuck to the bottom of the pan. Gently bring to the boil.

4   Once the sauce is boiling, remove it from the heat and use a hand blender to blitz it until smooth. (You can leave some of the peppers whole if you would like some added texture.)

5   Lift the pasta from the water using a slotted spoon and transfer it to the pan with the sauce (any residue of cooking water on the pasta water will help to thicken and combine the sauce). Stir the pasta until coated and serve straightaway, with an extra grinding of black pepper, if you wish.

potato & cauliflower biryani

This is the ideal midweek curry recipe. It freezes well so you can make it ahead of time and it uses the all-in-one method – so fewer dishes! Use large broccoli florets instead of cauliflower, if you prefer. If you like it spicy, add finely sliced fresh red chilli, too.

feeds 4 | 30min

olive oil, for frying
220g medium-sized
   cauliflower florets
350g peeled potatoes,
   cut into 1–2cm cubes,
   rinsed and patted dry
2 onions, finely sliced
3 tablespoons tomato
   purée
2 garlic cloves, finely
   chopped
½–1 teaspoon hot chilli
   powder
1 teaspoon ground
   turmeric
1 teaspoon ground cumin
1 teaspoon ground
   coriander
1 teaspoon curry paste
   (I use mild but a balti
   paste would work too)
900ml vegetable stock
350g basmati rice
small handful of
   coriander, roughly
   chopped, to serve
salt and freshly ground
   black pepper

1 Add a generous drizzle of oil to a large non-stick saucepan with a lid, and place on a medium heat. Add the cauliflower and potato and fry (without the lid) for 7 minutes, until just beginning to soften. Stir regularly, so the potato doesn't stick to the bottom of the pan.

2 Add the onions and fry for 5 minutes, until softened (add a little extra oil if needed).

3 Stir in the tomato purée, garlic, chilli powder, turmeric, cumin, ground coriander and curry paste. Fry for 1 minute, then stir in the vegetable stock, followed by the rice. Season with salt and pepper, stir once and bring the liquid to a rapid boil.

4 When the liquid is bubbling, place the lid on the pan and reduce the heat to low. Simmer for 10 minutes, until the rice is almost done, then remove the lid, stir and turn off the heat. Replace the lid, leaving it there for 5 more minutes, until the rice is cooked. Stir in the coriander and serve.

pea & asparagus risotto

This risotto is a bit of a cheat, to be honest. It doesn't even use risotto rice! The recipe gets all its creaminess from the combination of the excess stock and the soft cheese. It's a great timesaving hack and a lot easier to get right. You can swap the main ingredients for other vegetables and really make this risotto your own.

feeds 4 | 30min

olive oil, for frying
250g frozen peas
200g asparagus,
   trimmed and cut into
   3cm pieces
1 onion, finely chopped
2 cloves garlic, finely
   chopped
1 litre vegetable stock
350g basmati rice
30g parmesan cheese,
   finely grated, plus extra
   to serve
200g garlic and herb
   soft cheese
small handful of flat-leaf
   parsley, finely chopped,
   to serve (optional)
salt and freshly ground
   black pepper

1   Drizzle a little oil into a large, non-stick saucepan with a lid, and place on a medium-low heat. Add the frozen peas, asparagus and onion and fry (without the lid) for 10 minutes, stirring regularly, until the vegetables are tender. Add the garlic for the final 2 minutes of frying.

2   Add the stock to the pan and season with a little salt and pepper, then stir in the rice. Increase the heat and bring the liquid to the boil, then put the lid on the pan and turn the heat to low. Simmer for 10 minutes, stirring once halfway through cooking, until the rice is almost cooked.

3   Turn off the heat and, leaving the lid on the pan, leave the rice to steam for 5 minutes, or until cooked. Stir in both cheeses and finish with a little extra parmesan and some freshly ground black pepper. Sprinkle over some parsley, too, if you wish.

tip: If you want to make this entirely vegetarian, swap out the parmesan for some vegetarian Italian hard cheese.

sweet potato, feta & spinach pie

Unlike most of the recipes in this book, this one's a bit fiddly. It's not difficult, but you do need to give yourself a bit of time to put it together. It's absolutely worth it, though. The soft, sweet potato and feta, with the crunch of the filo pastry, is wonderful. Serve it with the Warm Bean Salad on page 215 or some carrot and cucumber sliced into ribbons and it's the perfect summer pie.

feeds 4-6 | 40min

750g sweet potatoes, peeled and cut into 2cm pieces
70g frozen spinach
3 tablespoons pine nuts
200g feta cheese, cut into 2cm cubes
50g butter
12 sheets of filo pastry
carrot and cucumber, sliced into ribbons, to serve (optional)
salt and freshly ground black pepper

1 Place the sweet potato in a saucepan with a lid and cover in boiling water. Place on a medium heat and bring the water back to the boil, then place the lid on the pan, reduce the heat, and simmer for 10 minutes, until the potato is tender. For the last minute, remove the lid, add the frozen spinach and stir until defrosted.

2 Drain the potato and spinach, return them to the pan and season with salt and pepper. Mash until the potato is roughly smooth with the spinach evenly distributed throughout.

3 Place the pine nuts in a dry non-stick frying pan roughly 25cm in diameter. Fry the nuts on a medium-low heat for about 1 minute, moving them around the pan until toasted. Stir the pine nuts into the potato mixture and set aside to cool a little, then stir in the feta cheese.

4 In the same frying pan, melt the butter on a low heat. Carefully pour the melted butter into a cup, leaving a thin layer of butter residue on the bottom of the pan.

5 Lay out a sheet of filo pastry on the worktop with one of the longest edges closest to you. Brush both sides, using the melted butter from the cup.

6 Butter a second sheet of pastry and lay it next to the first so they overlap by about a third. Butter another sheet of pastry and lay it in the centre above the first two sheets, so that it overlaps them by half. Repeat this process by laying 3 new buttered sheets of pastry over the first 3. Repeat the process one last time so that you have a triple layer of the sheets of pastry.

7   Carefully lift the layered pastry sheets and lay them in the buttered pan to cover the base. Allow the excess pastry to overhang the edge of the pan.

8   Tip the potato mixture into the pan and use a fork to spread it out, pressing it all the way into the edges. Fold the overhang of pastry over the top of the filling. Brush another 3 sheets of pastry with butter and layer these over the gaps on the top of the pie.

9   Place the pan on a medium heat and fry for 3–5 minutes, until the underside is golden (although don't worry if it's a bit pale at this stage), then cover the pan with a plate and carefully invert the pie on to it. The cooked side will now be on top.

10 Brush the pan with a little more butter. Carefully slide or lift the pie back into the pan, uncooked-side downwards, and fry for a further 3–5 minutes, until golden. If the top is still a little pale, repeat the process until both sides are crisp and golden.

11 Slide the pie on to a chopping board, cut into slices and serve immediately. Serve with carrot and cucumber ribbons, if you wish.

tip: Filo pastry dries out more quickly than other pastry. To make it easier to work with, only take it out of the fridge and packaging just before you need it, make sure your hands are dry and don't flour the worktop before you lay it down.

hob *a low simmer*

smoked haddock korma rice

This dish has a sweet, smoky flavour that is so moreish you'll never want it to end! Use mild curry powder if you're making it for the kids. You can serve with naan bread or salad, but I find that it's enough all by itself.

feeds 4 | 25min

olive oil, for frying
1 onion, finely chopped
small head of broccoli,
  broken into small–
  medium florets
140g baby corn, halved
  lengthways
1 tablespoon medium
  curry powder
1 x 400g tin of full-fat
  coconut milk
500ml vegetable stock
500g skinless, boneless
  frozen smoked haddock
  fillets, defrosted
180g basmati rice
handful of flat-leaf
  parsley, roughly
  chopped
naan breads or salad,
  to serve (optional)
freshly ground black
  pepper

1 Drizzle a little oil into a large saucepan with a lid, and place on a medium heat. Add the onion, broccoli and baby corn and fry (without the lid) for 5-7 minutes, stirring occasionally, until the onions have softened. Add the curry powder and fry for 1 minute, then stir in the coconut milk and stock. Gently bring to the boil on a medium-low heat.

2 Cut the haddock into bite-sized pieces. Add these to the pan along with the rice. Stir once and bring back to a gentle, rolling boil. Reduce the heat to low, stir once, and place the lid on the pan. Simmer for 10 minutes, or until the rice is cooked through.

3 Stir in the parsley, season with black pepper and serve with naan breads or salad, if you wish.

chicken goulash & herby potatoes

a low simmer

feeds 4 | 1h 15min

for the goulash
olive oil, for frying
600g skinless, boneless
   chicken thigh fillets, cut
   into bite-sized pieces
4 rashers of smoked
   bacon, cut into 2–3cm
   pieces
1 onion, roughly chopped
1 red pepper, deseeded
   and cut into bite-sized
   chunks
1 green pepper, deseeded
   and cut into bite-sized
   chunks
1 carrot, peeled and cut
   into thin slices
1 tablespoon plain flour
1–2 teaspoons smoked
   paprika (depending on
   how smokey you like it)
600ml chicken stock
a large handful of
   frozen peas
50ml soured cream
small handful of
   coriander, finely
   chopped, to serve
   (optional)
salt and freshly ground
   black pepper

for the herby potatoes
2 x 560g tins of peeled
   new potatoes, drained
   and rinsed
50g butter
1 tablespoon mixed herbs
   from a tube

This is basically a great-tasting chicken casserole. The chicken takes on all the flavours of the paprika and bacon, making the results deep and smoky. The recipe is a good way to use up the green peppers at the back of the fridge that are so tricky to find a good home!

I've used herbs from a tube rather than fresh, not only because it's more convenient, but also because it gives the goulash a lovely, vinegary tang.

1 Drizzle a little oil into a large saucepan on a medium heat. Add the chicken, bacon and onion and fry for 5 minutes, until the onion has softened and the chicken has taken on a bit of colour. Stir in both peppers, the carrot, flour and paprika and fry for 2 minutes, until you can no longer see any flour.

2 Stir in the stock, season with salt and pepper (go easy on the salt as the bacon adds a lot) and bring the liquid to the boil. Simmer, uncovered, on a low heat for 45 minutes, stirring occasionally, then increase the heat to high and simmer vigorously for a further 15 minutes, until the sauce has thickened and reduced.

3 In the meantime, 10 minutes before the goulash is ready, stir in the frozen peas and prepare the potatoes. First, cut any bigger potatoes in half and set aside.

4 In a large saucepan, melt the butter and the tablespoon of herbs together on a medium heat. When hot, add the potatoes and season with salt and pepper.

5 Reduce the heat to low and move the potatoes around the pan, so that they're coated in the herb butter and continue to heat through for 5–7 minutes.

6 When the goulash is ready, turn off the heat, stir in the soured cream and leave to rest for a few minutes before serving with the potatoes. Sprinkle with coriander, if you wish.

chicken & chorizo jambalaya

This is a family favourite in our house. It's an easy one-pan meal that virtually cooks itself. This is a kid-friendly dinner that I think will become a regular on your meal plan. If you want to up the veg, try adding broccoli florets to the pan with the onion and peppers.

feeds 4 | 35min

olive oil, for frying
500g chicken breast, cut into bite-sized pieces
1 onion, finely sliced
1 red pepper, deseeded and diced
1 yellow pepper, deseeded and diced
150g chorizo, thinly sliced into rings
1 tablespoon Cajun seasoning
1 x 400g tin of chopped tomatoes
750ml chicken stock
180g basmati rice
small handful of coriander, finely chopped, to serve (optional)
salt and freshly ground black pepper

1   Drizzle a little oil into a large saucepan with a lid, and place on a medium heat. When hot, add the chicken and fry (without the lid) for 5 minutes, stirring regularly, to seal the chicken all over. Remove the chicken from the pan and set aside on a plate.

2   Place the onion, both peppers and the chorizo in the pan with a little more oil. Fry for 5 minutes, until the vegetables are beginning to soften. Add the Cajun seasoning, fry for 1 minute, then return the chicken to the pan, with the tomatoes and stock. Season with salt and pepper and stir in the rice.

3   Bring the liquid to a vigorous boil on a medium heat. Stir once, then reduce the heat to low and place the lid on the pan. Simmer for 12 minutes. Remove the lid and simmer for 3 minutes, so that the sauce reduces and thickens. Check that the chicken is cooked through and the rice is tender. Serve in bowls, sprinkled with a little chopped coriander, if you wish.

tip: If you don't want to use chorizo, try using smoked bacon lardons instead; they'll give a lovely, but very different flavour.

hunter's stew

This stew is a meat-lover's dream! It's incredibly filling, so enough on its own, but you can make it go further by serving it with buttered crusty bread. Don't worry if the sausages break up a bit when the stew is simmering, it just adds to the rustic charm of the dish.

feeds 4–6 | 1h 45min

olive oil, for frying
handful of plain flour
900g boneless, skinless
  chicken thighs
8 Cumberland sausages
2 leeks, finely sliced
2 teaspoons dried
  mixed herbs
1 tablespoon balsamic
  vinegar
1 x 400g tin of chopped
  tomatoes
600ml chicken stock
600g potatoes, peeled
  and cut into 3–4cm
  pieces
small handful of flat-
  leaf parsley, roughly
  chopped, to serve
  (optional)
buttered crusty bread,
  to serve (optional)
salt and freshly ground
  black pepper

1 Pour a good glug of oil into a large saucepan with a lid, and place on a high heat. Add a little salt and pepper to the flour, before sprinkling over the chicken, turning until coated, then add the coated chicken to the pan and fry for 5 minutes, turning occasionally, until starting to brown. (You may have to do this in 2 batches.) Remove the chicken from the pan and set aside. Clean and dry the saucepan.

2 Place the sausages in the pan and arrange the leeks around them. Drizzle in a little more oil and fry for 10 minutes on a medium heat, turning regularly, until the sausages start to brown and the leeks have softened. The pan will be very crowded, but the leeks will quickly cook down to make turning the sausages easier.

3 Add the mixed herbs and balsamic vinegar, fry for 1 minute, then stir in the tomatoes, stock and fried chicken, and season with salt and pepper. Bring the liquid to the boil, then reduce the heat and place the lid on the pan. Simmer on low for 20 minutes, then remove the lid, stir in the potatoes and replace the lid. Simmer for a further 1 hour, stirring every 20 minutes or so, until the potatoes are tender and the chicken is cooked through. (Some of the sausage skins may come away from the sausages and rise to the top of the pan. Just discard as you go.)

4 Sprinkle with flat-leaf parsley, then divide between bowls and serve with buttered crusty bread on the side, if you like.

bbq pulled pork

This recipe will fill your house with wonderful smells all afternoon and will give you enough meat to feed a lot of people! Despite the length of time it takes to cook, it is a really easy dinner because it pretty much cooks itself. This is a perfect Sunday-night dinner.

fills 8–10 rolls | 5h

olive oil, for frying
1.8kg pork shoulder
2 garlic cloves, peeled
1 onion, finely sliced
1 litre chicken stock
1 teaspoon Dijon mustard
3 tablespoons tomato
* ketchup*
1 tablespoon balsamic
* vinegar*
1 tablespoon smoked
* paprika*
1 tablespoon light brown
* soft sugar*
1 tablespoon
* Worcestershire sauce*
salt and freshly ground
* black pepper*

to serve (optional)
lettuce leaves
slices of cucumber and
* tomato*
coleslaw (see page 166)
soft white rolls, halved

1 Pour a good couple of glugs of oil into a large saucepan with a lid, and place on a high heat. When hot, fry the pork (without the lid), skin-side downwards, for 10 minutes, until starting to brown. (Keep the string that holds the pork together attached.)

2 Add the whole cloves of garlic and finely sliced onion to the pan. Turn the heat down to medium and fry for another 5 minutes, stirring the onion regularly so it doesn't burn.

3 Turn the pork skin-side upwards and add the chicken stock until it covers about half of the meat (you may not need all the stock, or you may need to add a little more).

4 Bring the liquid to the boil and reduce the heat to its lowest setting. Place the lid on the saucepan and simmer the pork for 3 hours, checking every so often that the liquid level hasn't dropped (top it up with more stock if it has). After this time the pork should be tender enough to pull into larger pieces. Remove the lid and carefully remove the string from the pork. Pull the fat away from the meat – don't throw it away, you can make crackling from it.

5 Drain most of the stock from the pan, leaving about 200-300ml in there. If the garlic cloves are visible, remove them and discard them. Use 2 forks to pull apart the meat until you have big chunks. Add the Dijon mustard, ketchup, balsamic vinegar, paprika, sugar and Worcestershire sauce, and season with salt and pepper. Stir until the pork is coated. Place the lid back on the pan and return the mixture to a low simmer for 1-1½ hours, checking on it every 30 minutes or so. Each time you check, pull the pork apart a little more as it gets softer. The liquid should be reducing a little each time. If it seems to be reducing too quickly, make sure the heat is on its lowest setting and add a splash more stock.

6 Serve tucked into soft white rolls with salad and coleslaw, if you wish.

beef brisket & ale hotpot

Brisket is a great cut of beef. It's cheap and full of flavour. To get the best out of it, you need to cook it low and slow – perfect for a hotpot! I've swapped the traditional crispy potato topping for crispy bread and cheese. If the bread is too carb-heavy for you, though, a bowlful of the hotpot is still wonderful without it.

feeds 4 | 4h 30min

2 heaped teaspoons
   plain flour
800g beef brisket or beef
   roasting joint
olive oil, for frying
500ml beef stock
500ml pale or brown ale
2 carrots, peeled and
   sliced
1 onion, finely sliced
1 head of broccoli, broken
   into florets
large handful of
   frozen peas
1 small part-baked
   French loaf
30g butter
handful of finely grated
   cheddar cheese
small handful of flat-leaf
   parsley, finely chopped,
   to serve (optional)
salt and freshly ground
   black pepper

1   Season the flour with salt and pepper. Cut the mesh away from the beef joint and roll it in the flour until the beef has a light coating.

2   Drizzle a little oil into a large saucepan with a lid, and place on a medium heat. When hot, add the coated beef and fry (without the lid) for 5-7 minutes, turning regularly, until browned all over. Add the beef stock and ale, place the lid on the pan and simmer on the lowest heat for 3 hours, until the beef is just tender enough for you to use 2 forks to tear it apart into largish pieces.

3   Add the carrots, onion and broccoli, and season with salt and pepper. Simmer with the lid on for a further 30 minutes, until the vegetables are cooked.

4   Without the lid, tear the beef into smaller pieces and simmer on a medium-high heat, uncovered, for a further 20 minutes, until the sauce has thickened. Turn off the heat, stir in the frozen peas and leave the stew to rest while you prepare the topping.

5   Discard the ends of the part-baked bread. Cut the remainder into 1cm-thick slices, until you have enough to cover the bottom of a non-stick frying pan that is roughly the same size as the saucepan you used for the stew.

6   Without the bread in the pan, place the frying pan on a medium heat and add the butter, allowing it to melt and moving it around so that it coats the bottom of the pan. Place the slices of bread in the pan, quickly turning them over so that they're coated in butter on both sides. Fry for 2-3 minutes on each side, until toasted and golden brown, then remove from the pan and set aside.

7   Take the pan off the heat and sprinkle the cheese directly on to the bottom of the pan. Quickly return the bread to the pan, pressing it into the cheese.

8 Make sure all the bread is touching at least one other piece, so that you have a bread mosaic! Return the pan to a medium heat and, without moving the bread, allow the cheese to melt and then go golden brown, joining up the pieces of bread with a cheesy crust. (If there is cheese in the pan without bread on top of it, just gently push it towards the bread with a spatula as it melts.)

9 After 2 minutes, carefully lift up the corner of one of the bread slices to check that the cheese is lightly toasted. If it is, take the pan off the heat without moving the bread and leave it to cool in the pan and crisp up for 2 minutes. Turn out the cheesy bread crust on to a plate or chopping board. Carefully place the crust on top of the stew, cheese-side upwards, and serve, sprinkled with parsley, if you like.

chunky chipotle chilli beef

hob   a low simmer

feeds 4 | 2h 30min

olive oil, for frying
1 onion, finely chopped
400g beef chunks
small handful of
   plain flour
2 garlic cloves, finely
   chopped
1 teaspoon chipotle
   chilli flakes
1 teaspoon smoked
   paprika
1-2 teaspoons mild or hot
   chilli powder (depending
   on how spicy you like it)
1 teaspoon ground cumin
4 teaspoons beef gravy
   granules
2 teaspoons cocoa
   powder
2 teaspoons light brown
   soft sugar
boiling water, from
   a kettle
500g passata
200ml beef stock
2 x 400g tins of kidney
   beans, drained
salt and freshly ground
   black pepper

to serve
cooked white rice
soured cream (optional)
small handful of
   coriander, finely
   chopped (optional)

This is a thick, dark, smoky version of a chilli, that uses beef chunks rather than mince. It's really important to give it a little time to rest after cooking to allow the sauce to thicken and the beef to soften. Serve with rice and a dollop of soured cream.

1   Drizzle a little oil into a large saucepan with a lid on a medium heat. Add the onion and fry for 5 minutes, until softened.

2   Cut any larger beef chunks in half, so that you have equal-sized pieces, place them in a bowl, then sprinkle them with flour. Turn the beef until coated.

3   Add the beef and garlic to the pan and fry for 5 minutes on a low heat, stirring regularly, until the garlic is softened and the beef is browned.

4   In the meantime, mix together the chipotle chilli flakes, paprika, chilli powder, cumin, beef gravy granules, cocoa powder and sugar in a bowl and season with salt and pepper. Add just enough boiling water to turn the mixture into a thick, pourable sauce. Stir until smooth, adding a little more water if it becomes too thick as you stir.

5   Pour the sauce into the pan and fry for 1 minute, then stir in the passata and stock, making sure you gather up any spices that may be stuck to the bottom of the pan. Bring the liquid to the boil.

6   Place the lid on the pan, reduce the heat to its lowest setting and simmer for 1½ hours, removing the lid to stir occasionally. Then, stir in the kidney beans, replace the lid, and simmer for another 30 minutes, until the beef is cooked through and will pull apart easily.

7   Remove the lid, increase the heat to medium and simmer for 5 minutes to allow the sauce to thicken. Turn off the heat and leave the chilli to rest for 10 minutes before serving on a bed of rice, topped with a spoonful of soured cream and sprinkled with chopped herbs, if you wish.

midweek crowd pleasers

Packed with twists on classics, family favourites and easy wins when you're short on time, this chapter brims with recipes that will be on your meal plan week after week. These are the regular dinners to make the whole family happy.

chickpea, sweet potato & paneer curry

feeds 4-6 | **50**min

olive oil, for frying
225g paneer, cut into
 2-3cm cubes
1 onion, finely sliced
2 cloves garlic, finely
 chopped
1 teaspoon ground
 coriander
½ teaspoon mild or hot
 chilli powder (depending
 on how spicy you like it)
1 teaspoon ground
 turmeric
½ teaspoon tandoori
 spice
1 teaspoon ground cumin
500g passata
500ml vegetable stock
1 x 400g tin of chickpeas,
 drained
300g sweet potato,
 peeled and cut into
 3-4cm pieces
salt and freshly ground
 black pepper

to serve
small handful of
 coriander, roughly
 chopped
cooked rice or naan
 breads
shredded lettuce leaves
 (optional)

Paneer gives good texture to vegetarian curry dishes. If you've not cooked with it before, it's like a firmer, less salty feta cheese. It fries like halloumi and stays together through cooking. I serve it with rice (making it a two-pan meal), but if you want to save time, serve with naan bread and some shredded lettuce.

1 Drizzle a little oil into a large saucepan with a lid, and place on a medium-low heat. Add the cubed paneer and fry (without the lid) for 5 minutes, turning regularly, until golden brown all over. Remove from the pan and set aside on a plate.

2 Place the onion in the pan, add a little more oil if needed and fry on a medium heat for 7 minutes, until starting to colour and soften. Add the garlic, ground coriander, chilli powder, turmeric, tandoori spice and cumin and, stirring, fry for 1 minute, then stir in the passata, stock, chickpeas and sweet potato, and season with salt and pepper.

3 Bring the liquid to the boil, then turn the heat to low, placing the lid on the saucepan. Simmer for 15 minutes, stirring occasionally, until the chickpeas and sweet potato are beginning to soften.

4 Remove the lid, increase the heat to medium and simmer, stirring occasionally, for a further 15 minutes. Then, add the paneer and simmer for 5 minutes, until the sauce has thickened, the paneer is heated through and the sweet potato is completely soft. Serve sprinkled with coriander and with rice, or with naan bread and a little shredded lettuce if you wish.

tip: You can up the vegetable content of the curry by stirring in some fresh spinach at the end and gently wilting.

sweet potato, goat's cheese & onion naan bread

These are like lovely, doughy, sweet potato and goat's cheese pizzas. They're quick to make and the flavour combination is one of my favourites. This will feed four people for lunch or two for dinner, served with salad.

feeds **2** | **25**min

olive oil, for frying
3 onions, finely sliced
2 teaspoons balsamic
  vinegar
2 teaspoons runny honey
150g sweet potato
4 plain mini-naan breads
150g soft goat's cheese,
  thinly sliced into discs
side salad, to serve
salt and freshly ground
  black pepper

1   Drizzle a generous amount of oil into a non-stick saucepan on a medium-low heat. Add the onions and fry for 10 minutes, stirring regularly, until the onions are softened and coloured. Stir in the balsamic vinegar and honey, and season with salt and pepper. Turn the heat to low and fry for a further 5 minutes, until the mixture has reduced and is thick and sticky.

2   While the onions are frying, peel the sweet potato and cut it into very thin slices with a sharp serrated knife. If the potato is large, you may need to cut the slices in half as well.

3   Heat some oil in a separate non-stick frying pan (you'll need enough to just about cover the bottom). Add the sweet potato slices and fry for 5 minutes on a medium-low heat, turning occasionally, until soft. You need to ensure all the sweet potato slices are touching the bottom of the pan, so you may need to do this in batches. If cooking in batches, cover the first batch in foil to keep hot. Set the sweet potato aside.

4   Drain any excess oil from the frying pan, so that you're left with an oily coating. Reduce the heat to low and place 2 of the naan breads in the pan. Fry for 2 minutes on one side, then turn the naan breads over and top each with one quarter of the onions, spreading them out to the edges. Fry for a further 2 minutes, until the underside is golden.

5   Lay one quarter of the goat's cheese slices evenly over the onion layer on each naan bread. Move the naan bread to a chopping board and lay one quarter of the sweet potato slices evenly over the top of each. Finish with a little extra black pepper, then repeat the process for the other 2 naan breads and remaining onions, cheese and sweet potato. Serve with an extra grinding of black pepper, if you wish, and a salad on the side.

cajun chilli bean stew

This recipe is a cheap, tasty way to feed a lot of people as it's made mostly from tinned ingredients. The sweetness from the baked beans and the gentle heat from the Cajun spice makes it incredibly moreish. It uses two pans if you serve with rice, but I like flat breads for dunking.

feeds 4 | 30min

olive oil, for frying
1 onion, finely chopped
1 large red pepper,
   deseeded and finely
   chopped
1 tablespoon Cajun
   seasoning
½–1 teaspoon mild or hot
   chilli powder (depending
   on how spicy you like it)
2 garlic cloves, finely
   chopped
200ml vegetable stock
1 x 400g tin of chopped
   tomatoes
1 x 400g tin of baked
   beans
1 x 400g tin of 5-bean
   salad (choose one that
   includes sweetcorn),
   drained and rinsed
salt and freshly ground
   black pepper

to serve
cooked rice or flat breads
soured cream (optional)
small handful of
   coriander, roughly
   chopped (optional)

1   Drizzle a little oil into a large saucepan on a medium heat. Add the onion and pepper and fry for 5 minutes, until the vegetables have softened.

2   Add the Cajun seasoning, chilli powder and garlic and fry for a further 1 minute, then stir in the stock, tomatoes, baked beans and 5-bean salad, and season with salt and pepper.

3   Simmer on a low heat for 20 minutes, stirring occasionally, or until the sauce has reduced and thickened.

4   Serve with rice or flat breads, and with dollops of soured cream and a little chopped coriander and extra black pepper sprinkled over, if you wish.

tip: You can pack this stew out with more vegetables, such as broccoli, spinach or cauliflower to make it go even further.

cheesy-crumb fish pie

Fish pie is one of those midweek dinners that I love to eat but hate to cook. It's time consuming and creates a mountain of dishes. This recipe is a result of me trying to get all the flavours of a classic fish pie with less of the fuss. A far simpler version of a fish pie, it is just as tasty, but has a cheesy crumb instead of a potato topping. Think creamy fish and sauce with cheese on toast!

feeds 4–6 | 25min

80g butter
80g plain flour
800ml whole milk
100g frozen peas
100g frozen sweetcorn
150g frozen whole
   green beans
1 teaspoon Dijon mustard
   (or use English mustard
   if you want a bit more
   of a kick)
475g boneless skinless
   cod fillets (or any white
   fish), cut into bite-sized
   pieces
small handful of curly
   leaf parsley, roughly
   chopped, to serve
salt and freshly ground
   black pepper

for the topping
40g butter
3 slices of bread, cut into
   1cm cubes
handful of finely grated
   mature cheddar cheese

1 Melt the butter for the fish in a large, deep non-stick frying pan on a medium heat. If you don't have a suitable frying pan use a large saucepan. When melted, stir in the flour until it forms a thick paste.

2 On a medium heat, gradually add the milk, a little at a time, stirring continuously with a wooden spoon or whisk (to prevent lumps) and bringing the mixture gently to the boil before adding more milk. When you have added all the milk, stir in the frozen peas, sweetcorn, green beans and mustard.

3 Slowly bring the liquid back to the boil, stirring regularly, and simmer on a low heat for 3–5 minutes to soften the vegetables. Stir in the fish, season with salt and pepper and simmer for 5–7 minutes, until the fish is cooked through.

4 In the meantime, make the topping. Melt the butter in a separate non-stick frying pan on a medium heat. Add the bread cubes to the pan and stir to coat in the butter. Fry for 3–5 minutes, regularly moving the bread around the pan, until toasted.

5 Sprinkle over the cheese and leave for 1 minute to soften. Carefully turn the bread and cheese over and fry for 2 minutes, turning occasionally, until the cheese is completely melted and crisp.

6 Check the fish is cooked through, then sprinkle the cheesy toasts over the fish pie. Finish with some roughly chopped parsley and serve straightaway.

crispy fish wraps

feeds 4 | 25min

for the coleslaw
220g red cabbage,
   finely shredded
220g white cabbage,
   finely shredded
2 carrots, peeled and
   roughly grated
3 tablespoons soured
   cream
juice of 1 lime
1 teaspoon runny honey
1 tablespoon olive oil
salt and freshly ground
   black pepper

for the fish
110g plain flour
½ teaspoon baking
   powder
1 teaspoon salt
1 teaspoon freshly ground
   black pepper
160ml ice-cold
   sparkling water
1 x 380g bag of frozen
   skinless, boneless cod or
   Basa fillets, defrosted
olive oil, for frying

to serve
8 flour tortillas
cherry tomatoes, halved
   or quartered (optional)
sliced jalapeño from a jar
   (optional)
soured cream or
   mayonnaise (optional)
coriander (optional)

You could use fresh fish in this recipe, if you prefer, but using frozen not only makes it cheaper, but also makes it a useful standby dinner. Experiment with the coating: add spices to the flour to give the battered fish a bit of a kick, for example. If you're short on time, leave out the coleslaw and just serve the fish in wraps with salad.

1   First, make the coleslaw. Place the cabbages and carrots in a large mixing bowl and combine so that they're evenly distributed.

2   In a small bowl, mix together the soured cream, lime juice, honey and olive oil, and season with salt and pepper.

3   Pour the dressing over the vegetables, then use your hands to ensure everything is well coated in the dressing. Set aside. (You can make this ahead of time, then cover and refrigerate until needed, if you like.)

4   For the fish, put the flour in a large mixing bowl and stir in the baking powder, salt and pepper. Slowly add the sparkling water and whisk until smooth.

5   Cut the fish into medium-sized pieces, about the size of a chicken nugget. Pour the oil into a non-stick frying pan until you have about a 2mm depth all over the bottom of the pan. Heat the oil on a high heat until it starts to spit.

6   Dip each of the pieces of fish in the batter, then carefully place each piece in the hot oil. On a high heat, fry the fish pieces for 2 minutes each side, or until the batter is crispy and the fish is cooked through. (Depending on the size of your pan, you may have to do this in batches.) Remove from the pan with a slotted spoon and set aside on kitchen roll to absorb the excess oil.

7   To serve the wraps, place some of the coleslaw on a flour tortilla. Add some tomato and sliced jalapeño, if using, then place some pieces of the battered fish on top. Finish with a little extra soured cream or mayo, a sprinkle of coriander and a grinding of black pepper, if you like, then fold in half and eat!

chicken & mushroom stroganoff

This is the ideal dinner for busy days when time is short. The sauce is runny enough that you can happily serve it with pasta or rice for a truly hearty meal. The recipe requires two pans if served with pasta or rice.

feeds 4 | 25min

olive oil, for frying
1 onion, finely sliced
500g chicken breast, cut into bite-sized pieces
180g closed-cup mushrooms, sliced
1 tablespoon plain flour
1 teaspoon smoked paprika
1 teaspoon dried tarragon
300ml chicken stock
200ml soured cream
cooked rice or pasta, to serve (optional)
small handful of flat-leaf parsley, finely chopped, to serve (optional)
salt and freshly ground black pepper

1   Drizzle a little oil into a large, non-stick saucepan on a medium heat. Add the onion and chicken and fry for 5 minutes, until the chicken is sealed and starting to brown. Stir in the mushrooms and cook on a medium heat for 3-5 minutes, until they're soft and any liquid has evaporated. Stir in the flour, paprika and tarragon and fry for 1 minute, until you can no longer see any flour and it's starting to gently bubble.

2   Gradually add the stock, a little at a time, stirring continuously. Bring the liquid to the boil each time before adding more.

3   Stir in the soured cream, and season with salt and pepper. Bring the liquid to the boil and bubble on a hard simmer for 5-7 minutes, stirring regularly, until the sauce has reduced and thickened. Serve with pasta or rice, and sprinkle with parsley and an extra grinding of black pepper, if you wish.

tip: If you want to make this a little healthier, use reduced fat crème fraîche rather than soured cream.

creamy tandoori meatballs

This creamy meatball recipe has a spicy edge. You can use pork sausages, if you prefer, but I love the flavours of the chicken with the sauce. I always serve this with courgetti – courgettes sliced into 'spaghetti', using a spiraliser. Just divide the meatballs among four serving bowls and sauté the courgetti for a couple of minutes in olive oil, salt and pepper and the residue of the sauce left in the meatball pan. You can even add a few tomatoes on the vine at the same time.

feeds 4 | 25min

10 chicken chipolatas
   (see introduction, above)
handful of plain flour
olive oil, for frying
1 onion, finely sliced
1 red pepper, deseeded
   and finely sliced
1 yellow pepper, deseeded
   and finely sliced
2 teaspoons tandoori
   spice
300ml crème fraîche
   mixed with 100ml water
1 teaspoon freshly ground
   black pepper
large handful of spinach
lightly cooked courgetti
   and vine tomatoes, to
   serve (optional)
salt

1   Open the sausages by slicing the skin lengthways with a sharp knife. Discard the skins and tear each sausage into thirds.

2   Sprinkle the flour over a plate. Roll the sausage pieces in the palms of your hands to create balls, then roll them in the flour to coat.

3   Pour a good glug of oil into a large non-stick frying pan on a medium-high heat. When hot, add the meatballs and fry for 3–5 minutes, turning regularly, until sealed all over.

4   Add the onion and peppers to the pan with a little more oil and fry for 7 minutes, until softened. Add the tandoori spice and fry for 1 minute, then stir in the crème fraîche and water mixture. Add the pepper and season with salt.

5   Bring the liquid gently to the boil on a low heat, then add the spinach and simmer for a couple of minutes until wilted and the sauce has slightly thickened.

6   Check the meatballs are cooked through and serve with the courgetti and tomatoes, too, if you wish.

tuscan chicken

This is always a winner when we have friends over. The creamy, smoky flavours of the sauce when served with mashed potato makes the dish the ultimate comfort food! If you're serving with mashed potato or rice, you'll need two pans.

feeds 4–6 | **30**min

olive oil, for frying
4 large chicken breasts,
* halved lengthways*
* (or cut into thirds for*
* very thick breasts)*
1 onion, finely sliced
2 garlic cloves, finely
* chopped*
1 teaspoon paprika,
* plus extra to serve*
8–10 sundried tomatoes,
* cut into slivers*
300ml crème fraîche
50ml whole milk
large handful of spinach,
* shredded*
mashed potato or cooked
* rice, to serve*
salt and freshly ground
* black pepper*

1 Drizzle a little oil into a large, deep frying pan on a medium-high heat. Once hot, add the chicken and fry for 4–5 minutes on each side until sealed and starting to colour. Remove from the pan and set aside on a plate.

2 Place the onion in the pan with a little more oil and fry for 5 minutes, until softened. Add the garlic, paprika and sundried tomatoes. Fry for 1 minute, then stir in the crème fraîche and milk, and season with a generous grinding of salt and pepper. Add the shredded spinach and heat through on a gentle simmer for 2–3 minutes, until just bubbling.

3 Add the chicken to the sauce and simmer gently for 10 minutes, or until the chicken is cooked through. Finish with a sprinkling of black pepper and paprika and serve with mashed potato, or with rice if you prefer.

tip: If you're feeding a lot of people, double up on the ingredients and use diced chicken instead of whole breasts – it cooks quicker and will go further.

mongolian beef & crispy noodles

This is a simple, 25-minute fakeaway that tastes so good you'll be making it every week. The recipe makes two big portions and you can make it go further by adding extra vegetables, such as pak choi or sugar snap peas and serving it with rice.

feeds 2 | 25min

olive oil, for frying
bunch of spring onions,
  green and white parts
  cut into 2–3cm pieces
½ head of broccoli, cut
  into small–medium-sized
  florets
3 teaspoons beef gravy
  granules
1 teaspoon ground ginger
3 teaspoons dark
  soy sauce
3 teaspoons light brown
  soft sugar
200ml boiling water
small handful of
  plain flour
375g beef strips
2 garlic cloves,
  finely sliced
small handful of
  coriander, roughly
  chopped, to serve
  (optional)

for the noodles
300g straight-to-wok soft
  medium noodles
2–3 teaspoons cornflour
½ teaspoon salt
½ teaspoon freshly
  ground black pepper
vegetable oil, for frying

1 Spread the noodles out on a chopping board so they are roughly separated. This will allow them to dry out as you cook the beef.

2 Drizzle a little oil into a wok or large non-stick frying pan on a medium heat. Add the spring onions and broccoli florets and fry for 5 minutes, turning regularly, until the onions have softened.

3 While the spring onions and broccoli are cooking, in a bowl mix together the gravy granules, ginger, soy sauce, brown sugar and boiling water to a smooth sauce.

4 Sprinkle the flour over the beef strips, turning them over until they're coated, then add the beef to the wok and fry for 4 minutes, moving the beef around to ensure that it browns all over. Stir in the garlic for the final 1 minute, to soften.

5 Pour the sauce into the wok and allow it to heat up until bubbling. Reduce the heat to low and simmer for 3 minutes, stirring regularly, until the sauce has thickened a little and coated the ingredients.

6 While the beef is cooking, prepare the noodles. Mix the cornflour, salt and pepper together. Sprinkle the noodles with the seasoned flour, turning them over so they all have a light coating.

7 Divide the cooked beef mixture equally between 2 bowls and allow to rest while you cook the noodles.

8 Rinse and dry out the wok. Pour a good couple of glugs of oil into the wok and heat it on a high heat until spitting. Place the noodles in the wok and fry for 3–5 minutes, turning regularly with tongs or a fork, until golden and crisp.

9 Arrange the noodles over the beef and serve sprinkled with chopped coriander, if you wish.

lasagne(ish)

I love lasagne, but I hate the pile of dishes it creates and how long it takes to cook. This is a one-pan version that tastes just as good as the real thing, with half the fuss. Serve with salad.

feeds 4 | 35min

olive oil, for frying
1 onion, finely chopped
500g beef mince
1 garlic clove, finely
* chopped*
1 tablespoon tomato
* purée*
1 teaspoon dried oregano
1 x 400g tin of chopped
* tomatoes*
500ml beef stock
5 sheets of fresh lasagne
100g ricotta cheese
handful of grated mature
* cheddar cheese, plus*
* extra to serve*
small handful of flat-leaf
* parsley, finely chopped,*
* to serve (optional)*
salt and freshly ground
* black pepper*

1 Drizzle a little oil into a large, heavy-bottomed saucepan with a lid, and place on a medium heat. Add the onion and fry (without the lid) for 5 minutes, until softened.

2 Add the beef mince and fry for 5 minutes, stirring regularly, until browned. Add the garlic, tomato purée and oregano for the final 1 minute to soften the garlic a little.

3 Stir in the tomatoes and stock, and season with salt and pepper. Bring to the boil, then reduce the heat to low and simmer, uncovered, for 10 minutes, until the tomatoes have begun to break down and the sauce has thickened and reduced a little.

4 In the meantime, using scissors or a sharp knife, cut up the sheets of lasagne lengthways, each into 7 or 8 strips. Add the pasta strips to the sauce, stirring to distribute them evenly. Simmer on a low heat for 5 minutes, to soften.

5 In the meantime, beat the ricotta with a fork until smooth, then stir it into the sauce along with the cheddar. Place the lid on the pan, turn off the heat and leave to rest for 3 minutes.

6 Divide the mixture between 4 bowls and finish with a little more grated cheese, a grinding of black pepper and a sprinkling of chopped parsley, if you wish.

tip: You can use fresh tagliatelle instead of sliced lasagne sheets if you prefer.

big beef soup with horseradish croutons

If you've ever been of the opinion that soup is not a dinner because it's not filling enough, this one will change your mind. It's a comforting combination of beef and vegetables that when topped with the tangy croutons is a dinner you'll make again and again. If you don't like cabbage (or want to make the soup more kid-friendly), substitute frozen peas instead – just add them to the soup 10 minutes before serving. If you don't have time to make the croutons, just stir a little horseradish into the soup for an extra punch.

feeds 4–6 | 50min

olive oil, for frying
1 onion, finely sliced
large handful of shredded
   sweetheart or savoy
   cabbage
400g diced beef
handful of plain flour
2 garlic cloves, finely
   sliced
1.4 litres beef stock
1 carrot, peeled and sliced
400g potatoes (any are
   fine), peeled and cut
   into 3cm chunks
½ teaspoon Marmite
salt and freshly ground
   black pepper

for the croûtons
40g butter
3 teaspoons horseradish
   sauce
2 slices of bread, cut into
   2–3cm cubes

1   Drizzle a little oil into a large saucepan with a lid, and place on a medium heat. Add the onion and cabbage and fry (without the lid) for 5 minutes, until the onion is softened.

2   Cut any larger beef chunks in half, so that you have equal-sized pieces. Place them in a bowl, sprinkle in the flour and turn the beef until coated.

3   Add the floured beef and the garlic to the pan with a little more oil and fry for 5 minutes, stirring regularly so the beef doesn't stick to the pan, until browned all over.

4   Stir in the stock, carrot, potatoes and Marmite, and season with salt and pepper. Bring the liquid to the boil, then reduce the heat, place the lid on the pan and simmer on low for 40 minutes, until the carrots and potato are tender. Taste the soup and add a little more Marmite or seasoning if required.

5   In the meantime, 10 minutes before the soup is ready, prepare the croûtons. Mix the butter and horseradish sauce together in a non-stick frying pan on a low heat, stirring until melted and bubbling. Add the bread cubes and stir to coat.

6   Fry the bread for 4–5 minutes on a medium heat, moving it around the pan continuously, until toasted. Season with black pepper (no need for salt).

7   Serve the soup in bowls and place the croûtons in the middle of the table so people can help themselves.

sausage & leek ragù

This one's a proper, hearty one-pan meal that's perfect when you're cooking for guests. Chicken chipolatas work well if you fancy a change from pork.

feeds 4–6 | 1h 15min

30g butter
2 leeks, finely sliced
2 carrots, peeled and
  diced
400g Cumberland
  sausages
2 garlic cloves, finely
  chopped
1 x 400g tin of chopped
  tomatoes
1 litre chicken stock
270g fusilli or penne
  pasta
handful of flat-leaf
  parsley, finely chopped,
  to serve
salt and freshly ground
  black pepper

1   Melt the butter in a large non-stick saucepan with a lid on a medium heat. (I use a cast-iron casserole pan.) Add the leeks and carrots. Fry (without the lid) on a low heat for 10 minutes, stirring regularly, until the vegetables are soft.

2   Use a knife to slit the skins of the sausages. Pull out the meat and discard the skins. Tear each piece of sausage meat into 5 smaller pieces and place these in the pan, along with the garlic. Increase the heat to medium and fry for 7 minutes, stirring regularly, to ensure the sausage meat doesn't stick to the bottom of the pan. Stir in the tomatoes and stock, and season with salt and pepper. Bring the liquid to the boil, then reduce the heat to low.

3   Place the lid on the pan and simmer the ragù for 30 minutes, removing the lid to stir a couple of times during cooking, until the carrots have softened and the tomatoes have begun to break down.

4   Remove the lid and stir the pasta into the sauce. Bring the mixture to the boil and simmer (without the lid) on a medium heat for 10 minutes, stirring once or twice during cooking.

5   Reduce the heat, place the lid on the pan and simmer on low for a further 5 minutes, or until the pasta is tender. Turn off the heat and leave to rest for 5 minutes with the lid on. Stir through the parsley and serve.

tip: If you want to freeze this, just make it up to the point before you add the pasta. Then, when you need it, defrost, heat through and continue with the recipe above.

sweet hob

Simple sweet treats, show-stopping cakes and divine pan shares – whether you're looking for a quick after-dinner fix or a long, relaxing weekend 'bake', you'll find just what you need right here, from the hob.

apple & cinnamon rolls

Chances are you'll already have the ingredients to make these. Sweet cinnamon apples in a thin, crisp crust, they taste just like a popular fast-food restaurant's apple pie! They're quite small so you can fry several at the same time.

makes 4 | 20min

2 eating apples, cored
  and cut into 1cm cubes
  or pieces (skin left on)
2 tablespoons caster
  sugar, plus a little extra
  to sprinkle
1 teaspoon ground
  cinnamon
4 slices of thick, white
  farmhouse bread, crusts
  removed
30g butter

1   Place the apple pieces in a small pan with the sugar, cinnamon and 1 tablespoon water. Simmer for 10 minutes on a medium-low heat, stirring regularly, until the apple pieces have softened but are still holding their shape. Add a splash more water if they are drying out too quickly.

2   In the meantime, use a rolling pin to roll the bread out as thinly as you can, leaving you with flat rectangles.

3   Melt the butter in a non-stick frying pan. Once melted, take it off the heat. Brush both sides of the bread with melted butter, all the way to the edges. Keep the remaining melted butter.

4   Divide the cooked apple mixture between the slices of bread, spreading it down the centre of the length of each flattened slice. Taking a short end, tightly roll the apple up in the bread, pressing each rolled slice down a little to hold it in place and keeping the join underneath.

5   Reheat the remaining butter in the pan on a medium-low heat. Place the rolls, with the join facing downwards, in the pan and fry for 4-5 minutes. Turn the rolls until they are golden brown and crisp all over. Adjust the heat if they are cooking too fast. Sprinkle with a little sugar and serve.

tip: These are quite small, so if you're feeding a few – make a double batch! You can experiment with different fruit. Try mixing blackberries in with the apples as they're cooking.

banana & peanut butter pancakes

This recipe works just a well as a breakfast as it does a dessert – fluffy, bouncy American-style pancakes that are great on their own, and even better served with honey! There isn't a strong flavour of peanut butter, just a nutty background taste.

makes 10 small pancakes | 20min

2 ripe bananas, peeled
2 eggs
2 heaped tablespoons
  smooth peanut butter
1 x 400g tin of rice
  pudding
1 dessertspoon caster
  sugar
150g plain flour
butter, for frying
runny honey (optional)

1 Break the bananas into a mixing bowl and mash with a fork until smooth.

2 Beat the eggs into the banana, then whisk in the peanut butter, rice pudding, sugar and flour. Make sure all the ingredients are thoroughly combined.

3 Melt a knob of butter in a large non-stick frying pan on a medium heat and ladle in 2 or 3 separate puddles of the mixture so that you can cook 2 or 3 pancakes at a time. Fry on a medium heat for 2-3 minutes on each side, until golden all over. Repeat until you have used all the batter.

4 Remove to a serving plate, drizzle over a little honey and serve.

tip: Try adding a teaspoon of jam to the pancake when you first add it to the pan. Carefully swirl it through the batter and you'll have a lovely jammy spiral running through your pancakes!

pan-share blackberry crumble

You can use fresh blackberries for this one-pan treat, but I like to use frozen as they hold together better in the pan. The topping has a sweet, chewy, nutty taste that goes perfectly with the sharp blackberries and a dollop of vanilla ice cream.

feeds 2–3 | 20min

375g frozen blackberries
2 dessertspoons light
  brown soft sugar
scoops of vanilla
  ice cream, to serve
  (optional)

for the topping
60g unsalted mixed nuts
30g light brown soft
  sugar
40g plain flour
30g butter

1 First, make the topping. With a pestle and mortar or the end of a rolling pin, roughly crush the nuts into very small pieces. Stir in the sugar and flour.

2 Melt the butter in a large, non-stick frying pan on a medium heat. Add the nut mixture and reduce the heat to low. Stir until all the ingredients are coated in butter, then gently fry for 5 minutes, stirring continuously, until the nuts are lightly toasted and the sugar has melted.

3 Pour the topping into a bowl and set aside. It will crisp as it cools.

4 Make the filling. Add the still-frozen blackberries to the pan on a medium heat and sprinkle with the brown sugar. Simmer the blackberries gently for 10 minutes, stirring regularly until they're soft and heated through and the pan has a covering of juice.

5 Turn off the heat. Sprinkle the nutty topping over the blackberries, breaking it up with your hands as you go. Serve topped with scoops of ice cream, if you wish.

tip: Using frozen blackberries means that it is easy to rustle up a last-minute throw-together dessert, perfect for when you're busy.

s'mores' hash

This is an indoor version of an American camping classic – although it may not be for you if you don't have a sweet tooth. It is definitely not one for the faint-hearted! Think gooey melt of all the s'mores' ingredients, cooked in a pan. A sure hit when we have a group of kids over, it's a great dessert to have outdoors after a barbecue.

feeds 6 | 10min

15 rich tea biscuits, each broken into 3 or 4 pieces
25g butter
25 medium-sized marshmallows (about 200g)
50ml double cream or crème fraîche
150g milk chocolate, broken into squares

1 Add the biscuits, butter and marshmallows to a large non-stick frying pan. On a low heat, gently warm the mixture for 3 minutes, turning it over regularly with a spatula. The butter will melt and the marshmallow will begin to soften.

2 Place the cream and chocolate in a bowl and mix until the chocolate is thoroughly coated in cream. Add the cream and chocolate to the pan. Gently keep turning the mixture for 2-3 minutes, still on a low heat, or until the chocolate is soft and beginning to melt and the marshmallow has become gooey. Serve immediately in bowls.

fried cookie dough

For this recipe you'll need a heavy-bottomed frying pan with great non-stick credentials. The difference between this cookie and oven-baked ones is that you'll get a soft, gooey centre with a lightly crisped outside. Firm enough to cut into slices, but soft enough to eat with a spoon!

feeds 4 | 30min

125g margarine or
  spreadable butter
70g caster sugar
1 egg, beaten
40g mixed unsalted nuts
250g plain flour, plus
  extra for dusting
50g 70% dark chocolate,
  roughly chopped into
  small pieces (or use
  chocolate chips if
  you prefer)
1 scoop vanilla ice cream,
  to serve (optional)

1 Cream the margarine and sugar together in a mixing bowl until pale and fluffy, then stir in the beaten egg.

2 Use a pestle and mortar or the end of a rolling pin to bash the nuts into smaller pieces (don't be tempted to use a food processor as the pieces will be too fine). Stir the nuts and flour into the batter until you have a smooth, slightly sticky dough.

3 Divide the dough roughly into 2 balls. Place one of the dough balls onto a flour-dusted worktop and press it into a circle with your fingers, roughly 15cm wide.

4 Break the chocolate into squares and, using a heavy knife, cut each square into 3 or 4 pieces. Scatter the chocolate pieces evenly over the dough circle.

5 Press the other dough ball into an identical-sized circle and lay it over the top of the first, gently pressing them together and sandwiching the chocolate pieces in between.

6 Heat a 20cm-wide, heavy-bottomed non-stick pan (I use a cast iron pan) on a medium-low heat. When hot, place the dough circle in the pan and gently press it into the edges. You should hear a quiet, gentle sizzle as it fries. If it sounds like it's frying too furiously, turn the heat down a little. After 4 minutes lay a plate over the pan and place your hand on top of the plate. Holding the handle of the pan, carefully turn the whole thing over, turning the cookie out onto the plate. Use a metal fish slice to slide it back into the pan so the cooked side is now on top. Don't worry if it falls apart a little, just use the metal slice to press it together and into the sides of the pan again. Cook for 3 minutes, then repeat the process of turning it out onto a plate.

7 Leave the cookie to cool and firm up for 10 minutes. Cut into slices and serve topped with a scoop of ice cream.

crêpes & strawberry cream

It took me a long time to perfect my pancake recipe – and these are thin, light and lovely every time. Make the strawberry cream a few hours before you need it, to give it time to chill in the fridge.

makes 5-6 | 30min

for the strawberry cream
400g strawberries
3 teaspoons icing sugar
150ml double cream

for the pancakes
2 eggs
300ml whole milk
100g plain flour
pinch of salt
butter, for frying

1 First, make the strawberry cream. Reserve 2 or 3 whole strawberries for garnishing, then hull the remainder and cut them into 2cm pieces. Place the strawberry pieces in a non-stick saucepan and sprinkle in the icing sugar. Cook on the lowest heat for 5 minutes, stirring regularly, until the strawberries have released their juice and it has become thick and syrupy. Place the strawberries and the juice in a bowl and leave to cool completely.

2 Place the cream in a mixing bowl and, using an electric hand whisk, whisk until it holds firm peaks.

3 When the strawberries are cool, beat them (with the syrup) into the cream with a wooden spoon, cover and place in the fridge.

4 Make the pancakes. Whisk the eggs and milk together in a large mixing bowl. Sift the flour into the bowl with a pinch of salt, then fold them into the egg mixture and whisk until smooth.

5 Heat a knob of butter in a non-stick frying pan on a medium heat. Move the melted butter around the pan to coat the base.

6 Ladle batter into the pan - just enough so that when you tilt the pan, the batter just covers the base. Fry on a medium heat for 2 minutes on each side, or until the bottom of the pancake is cooked and comes away easily. Repeat until you have used up all the batter. Serve with the strawberry cream and slices of the reserved whole strawberries.

tip: If you have any leftover strawberry cream, place it in a small, covered container and freeze it. You'll have a quick strawberry ice cream!

pineapple turnovers

If, like me, you always have a tin of pineapples lurking at the back of your cupboard, this is the four-ingredient recipe for you. If you've never used filo pastry, don't be put off. It's easy to work with, just make sure you get it out of the fridge only when you need it, as it dries out quickly.

makes 5 | 30min

1 x 432g tin of pineapple
  chunks
1 dessertspoon caster
  sugar, plus a little extra
  to sprinkle
50g butter, plus extra if
  needed
5 sheets filo pastry

1 Drain the pineapple, reserving 4 tablespoons of juice from the tin. Cut the pineapple chunks into 3 or 4 pieces. Place them in a non-stick frying pan and add the sugar and reserved juice. Place over a medium heat and bring the liquid to the boil.

2 Simmer for 7-10 minutes, stirring regularly, until the pineapple is soft and the sauce is thick and syrupy. Transfer the pineapple and sauce to a bowl to cool.

3 Melt the butter in the same pan (don't worry if there's still a little pineapple juice in the bottom) on a medium heat, then pour into a cup. You should be left with a very thin layer of butter in the pan.

4 Lay the pastry on your work surface, so that a long side runs left to right in front of you. Brush both sides of the pastry with butter, right up to the edges. Fold one third of the long end of the pastry towards the centre and do the same for the other end, overlaying the first fold as if you were folding a business letter, so that you have a triple-layered piece of pastry.

5 With a short edge closest to you, place 1 dessertspoon of the pineapple a few centimetres in from the bottom of the strip.

6 Hold the bottom left hand corner of the pastry and carefully lift it diagonally over the pineapple, until it joins to the right-hand side of the pastry, giving you a triangle.

7 Press the edges of the pastry together and carefully move the filling around the inside of the triangle so it goes into all 3 corners.

8 Fold the filled triangle upwards, onto the filo rectangle. Continue folding the triangle upwards until you have used up all the pastry. You should be left with a small flap at the end; fold that over the triangle to seal the final edge. Repeat with the remaining pastry sheets and filling.

9 Pour any remaining butter back into the pan and heat until sizzling.

10 Fry the turnovers on a medium-low heat for 3-4 minutes on each side until crisp and golden brown. (Add more butter if the pan dries out.) Sprinkle with a little sugar and leave to cool for a few minutes before eating. They stay hot in the centre for a very long time.

chocolate oat biscuits

This is my favourite version of a chocolate flapjack. These biscuits taste wonderful and make a lovely, lazy weekend 'bake' that is perfect if you're looking for something to make with the kids. They're super quick to prepare with only 10 minutes hands-on time, but need 3 hours to firm up in the fridge.

makes 8–10 | 3h 15min

150g milk chocolate,
  broken into squares
100g butter
2 tablespoons milk
  (any is fine)
3 tablespoons runny
  honey
85g mixed unsalted nuts
1 eating apple, roughly
  grated (skin on)
325g porridge oats

1   Grease and line a roughly 28cm x 20cm baking tin or dish.

2   Place the chocolate, butter, milk and honey in a large saucepan. Gently heat for 2 minutes, stirring continuously on a low heat, or until the mixture has melted together and combined. Set the chocolate aside.

3   Break the nuts into small pieces with the end of a rolling pin or in a pestle and mortar.

4   Add these to the pan along with the grated apple and porridge oats and turn the heat right down to its lowest setting. Spend 2–3 minutes working the ingredients through each other, until they're thoroughly combined and the oats are coated in chocolate.

5   Spoon the mixture into the prepared tin or dish, using the back of a spoon to press it down firmly, working around the edges to ensure that it's compacted and level. Leave to cool, then place the tray in the fridge for at least 3 hours for the mixture to firm up.

6   Remove the biscuit from the tray and cut into equal-sized pieces.

tip: These make ideal lunchbox fillers. Freeze a batch by putting the biscuits between sheets of greaseproof paper so that they don't stick together. You can take them out of the freezer individually when you need them.

steamed bakewell pudding

When I was little, my dad would often make a steamed pudding on Sunday. It was always a bit of a labour of love, but *always* worth it. This one's the same. It takes a bit of time to cook, but if you're in the mood for a Sunday treat, you'll never regret making it. It has all the flavours of a Bakewell tart in a comforting pudding.

feeds 6 | 2h 15min

100g self-raising flour
100g ground almonds
1 teaspoon baking powder
170g caster sugar
170g unsalted butter
3 eggs, beaten
couple of drops of almond extract
3 tablespoons raspberry jam
100g icing sugar

1 Line a 450g loaf tin. Combine the flour, ground almonds and baking powder in a mixing bowl.

2 In a separate bowl, cream the sugar and butter until pale and fluffy, then stir the beaten egg and almond extract, and mix until smooth. Add the dry ingredients to the wet ingredients and beat with a wooden spoon until thoroughly combined, then pour into the loaf tin.

3 Put the jam in a cup and mix vigorously until it's loosened and easy to spread. Spoon the jam into the cake mixture in several places and use a narrow knife to make figures of eight in the batter, giving you a jammy marble effect.

4 Place a small metal dish or trivet in the bottom of a large saucepan with a lid. Check that it fits by placing the trivet, loaf tin and lid on the pan. If you don't have a lid, just cover the top of the pan with a metal baking tray or piece of foil to trap in the steam.

5 Cover the loaf tin with foil and secure by tying string around the rim of the tin. Place the tin on the trivet and pour boiling water into the pan until it reaches halfway up the sides of the loaf tin.

6 Place the pan on a medium heat and bring the water back to the boil. Place the lid on the pan and turn the heat down to its lowest setting. Simmer for 2 hours, topping up the water if it needs it.

7 To check the pudding is cooked, insert a knife into the centre. If it comes out clean, the pudding is done. Leave to cool for 2 minutes in the tin, then carefully turn it out onto a plate and leave to cool.

8 Meanwhile, place the icing sugar in a bowl and add 3 teaspoons water. Mix quickly until smooth. When the pudding is completely cool, drizzle generously with icing and serve.

squidgiest chocolate brownies

My brownies used to turn out dry and often stuck to the bottom of the pan. These brownies are guaranteed squidgy and moist every time. The cooking time on this is a little longer than oven-cooked brownies, but your window for cooking them to perfection is so much wider. Hands-on time is only a few minutes – once the brownie mixture is in the pan it's very low maintenance.

makes 8 large brownies | 1h 30min

120g butter
120g 70% dark chocolate, broken into squares
200g caster sugar
3 eggs
100g plain flour
2 tablespoons cocoa powder
whipped cream or crème fraîche, to serve (optional)

1   Line a small metal baking tray that will fit inside your frying pan. It should be about 25cm x 20cm and 5–6cm deep. If you don't have baking paper, grease the tin and sprinkle a little flour around the edges. Tap off the excess flour.

2   Put the butter and chocolate into a large, deep, non-stick frying or sauté pan. Gently heat until both are melted. Leave to cool a little in the pan.

3   Place the sugar and eggs in a mixing bowl and, using an electric hand whisk, whisk for about 5 minutes, or until the mixture is milkshake thick and has nearly doubled in size.

4   Sift the flour and cocoa powder into the fluffy eggs, then fold in the melted chocolate, using a wooden spoon or spatula, until fully combined and no streaks remain. Take care not to knock the air out of the mixture.

5   Rinse out the frying pan and return it to the hob. Tip the brownie mixture into the prepared tin, making sure it's evenly spread out. Cover the tin with foil, scrunching it down around the edges to seal.

6   Place the tin in the pan and pour in boiling water so that it reaches three-quarters of the way up the sides of the tin. Cover the pan with a lid, tin foil or a metal tray to keep the steam in.

7   Simmer the water on a low heat for 1 hour and 10 minutes until the brownie is cooked through and the centre is firm and springy. Top up the water level every so often.

8   Leave the brownie to rest in the tray for 5 minutes before cutting into squares and leave to cool before serving with whipped cream or crème fraîche, if you wish.

toasted brioche & hippy blueberry jam

This is a favourite with my kids. It works just as well as an after-school treat as it does as a dessert, or even breakfast. Toasting the brioche in the pan makes it soft, sweet and pudding-like and the results are perfect for lazy weekends. I call this hippy jam, because unlike regular jam, which takes time, precision and thermometers, this one is a much more laid-back affair!

feeds 2-4 | 20min

150g blueberries
3 teaspoons caster sugar
squeeze of lemon juice
40g butter
4 slices of brioche, from a loaf

1   Place the blueberries in a large non-stick frying pan with the sugar and lemon juice. Cook on a low heat for 5-7 minutes, stirring and squashing the blueberries with a wooden spoon, until you have a thick jam consistency. Spoon the jam into a bowl and leave to cool.

2   Rinse and dry the frying pan. Return the pan to the hob and add half the butter. Place on a medium-low heat and allow to melt and heat up.

3   When the butter is hot, place 2 slices of brioche in the pan and quickly turn them over so that both sides are coated in butter. Fry the bread for 1-2 minutes on each side, pressing the bread down gently as it fries, until golden. Repeat with the remaining butter and brioche slices.

4   Drizzle the jam over and serve.

tip: Try swapping the blueberries for raspberries for another quick 'jam'.

simple sides

Most of the recipes in this book are complete meals. Where they're not, I've made a serving suggestion. I have included five simple sides in this section that will work with several of the recipes.

jerk sweet potato

Sweet and spicy, this side is easy and filling. It's a great alternative to any potato dish.

feeds 4 | 20min

850g sweet potato, cut
  into 1-2cm pieces
boiling water from a
  kettle, plus an extra
  50ml
vegetable oil, for frying
1 onion, finely sliced
2 garlic cloves, finely
  chopped
2 tablespoons soy sauce
2 tablespoons light brown
  soft sugar
1 teaspoon mild or hot
  chilli powder (depending
  on how spicy you like it)
½ teaspoon allspice
salt

1 Place the sweet potato in a large saucepan with a lid and cover in boiling water from the kettle. Place on a high heat and bring to the boil. Turn the heat to a lowish setting and simmer for 5 minutes, or until the potato is tender. Drain the potato in a colander and leave to steam dry for a minute or two.

2 Drizzle a little oil into the pan on a medium heat. Add the onion and fry for 5 minutes, stirring regularly, until softened.

3 In the meantime, in a bowl, mix together the garlic, soy sauce, sugar, chilli powder and allspice. Season with salt and stir in the 50ml of boiling water to make a sauce.

4 Add the sauce to the onions and fry for 2 minutes. Stir in the sweet potato, mixing until thoroughly coated. Gently heat through for 1 minute and serve.

tip: Use spring onions instead of onion, if you prefer, and add a squeeze of lime for an extra punch of flavour.

creamy mashed potato

It might seem odd that I've included a recipe as simple as mashed potato. But the difference between okay mash and great mash is huge! I've worked out the quantities and technique that will give you the perfect amount of creamy, fluffy mash, every time.

feeds 4 **|** 30min

*1.3kg potatoes (any type
– I use baking), peeled
and cut into 4–5cm
pieces
about 1 teaspoon salt
100ml whole milk
100g butter
freshly ground black
pepper*

1   Place the potato pieces in a large saucepan with a lid. Fill the saucepan with cold water, then drain. Do this a couple of times to wash the starch off the potatoes (until the drained water runs clear).

2   Fill the pan with cold water to cover the potatoes and salt the water with about 1 teaspoon of salt. Place the pan on a medium heat and bring the water to the boil. When boiling, turn the heat to low and place the lid on the pan.

3   Simmer the potatoes for around 15 minutes, or until they are tender enough to cut in half easily with a knife, then drain the potatoes and allow to steam in the dry pan or in the colander for 1 minute.

4   Use a fork to mash the potatoes – spend a bit of time crushing them until they're nearly lump free, then use a potato masher to go over the potato, getting rid of the last few lumps. The longer you do this for, the smoother your mash will be.

5   Add the milk. Use a wooden spoon to beat the milk into the potato to start to make it fluffy.

6   Add the butter and season generously with salt and pepper, then continue to beat until the butter has melted and the mash is smooth and creamy. Keep warm until you're ready to serve.

spiced rice

You can play around with the spices in this – try tandoori or Cajun as alternatives. This works well cold as a rice salad at a picnic or barbecue.

feeds 4 | 15min

vegetable oil, for frying
1 onion, finely chopped
3 tablespoons tomato
   ketchup
½–1 teaspoon mild or hot
   chilli powder (depending
   on how spicy you like it)
1 teaspoon ground
   turmeric
1 teaspoon ground cumin
120ml boiling water
100g drained, tinned
   sweetcorn
150g drained, tinned
   kidney beans
2 x 250g pouches of
   cooked long grain rice
salt and freshly ground
   black pepper

1 Drizzle a little oil into a large non-stick saucepan over a medium heat. Add the onion and fry for 5 minutes, until softened.

2 In the meantime, in a bowl, mix together the ketchup, chilli, turmeric, cumin and boiling water to make a sauce.

3 Pour the sauce over the onions and simmer for 1 minute, then stir in the sweetcorn and kidney beans.

4 Crumble the rice into the pan so that they are mostly individual grains. Stir on a medium heat until the rice is coated. Break up any remaining clumps of rice with a wooden spoon as you stir.

5 Turn the heat to its lowest setting, place the lid on the pan and simmer for 5–7 minutes, stirring occasionally and adding a splash of water if the pan looks like it's drying out, until the rice is heated through. Season with salt and pepper and serve.

tip: This is also a great way to use leftover cooked rice if you have any; just add it instead of packet rice and make sure it's fully heated through.

from the top: warm bean salad (see page 215), spiced rice (see page 212), jerk sweet potato (see page 210)

steamed spinach & cashews

Spinach is a lovely side. It's quick and easy to cook, but often not very exciting. By adding just a few extra ingredients, you can make something very simple, taste incredible.

feeds 2 | 10min

25g butter
2 garlic cloves, finely
  chopped
½ teaspoon ground
  nutmeg
200g fresh spinach
15g unsalted cashews,
  roughly crushed, to serve
salt and freshly ground
  black pepper

1   Melt the butter in a large saucepan on a low heat. Add the garlic and fry gently for 2 minutes, until softened. Stir in the nutmeg, fry for 1 minute, then add the spinach and turn the heat down to its lowest setting.

2   Stir the spinach continuously, coating it in butter and garlic. When it has just wilted remove it from the heat. Season with salt and pepper.

3   Use tongs to lift the spinach from the pan into a bowl. This will help to squeeze out a little of the excess moisture. Sprinkle the crushed cashews over the top and serve immediately.

warm bean salad

This bean salad makes a great lunch as well as a delicious side. Add extra vegetables or leftovers to make a meal of it, or serve it with chicken or fish fillets.

feeds 4 | 10min

vegetable oil, for frying
1 onion, finely chopped
60ml olive oil
20ml balsamic vinegar
1 teaspoon Dijon mustard
1 teaspoon runny honey
handful of flat-leaf
  parsley, finely chopped
2 x 400g tins of mixed
  beans in water, drained
170g drained, tinned
  sweetcorn
salt and freshly ground
  black pepper

1 Drizzle a little oil into a large saucepan with a lid and place on a medium heat. Add the onion and fry for 5 minutes, until softened.

2 While the onion is frying, make a sauce by combining the olive oil, balsamic vinegar, mustard, honey and parsley in a bowl. Whisk with a fork until smooth, and season with salt and pepper.

3 Pour the sauce into the pan and add the beans and sweetcorn. Reduce the heat to low and stir to combine, then simmer for 3 minutes.

4 Place the bean salad in a bowl and leave to cool a little. Season with a little more salt and pepper and serve warm to allow the dressing to absorb into the beans and sweetcorn.

tip: Swap the balsamic vinegar for white wine vinegar and you have an easy French dressing that you can use on any salad.

index

meal planner

master meal plan   2-month plan

quick
dinners

budget

weekend
food

family
favourites

something
new

master meal plan

quick dinners

budget

weekend food

family favourites

something new

meal planner   wk___

	breakfast	lunch	dinner	snacks
monday				
tuesday				
wednesday				
thursday				
friday				
saturday				
sunday				

shopping list

- [ ]
- [ ]
- [ ]
- [ ]
- [ ]
- [ ]
- [ ]

meal planner   wk___

	breakfast	lunch	dinner	snacks
monday				
tuesday				
wednesday				
thursday				
friday				
saturday				
sunday				

shopping list

- [ ]
- [ ]
- [ ]
- [ ]
- [ ]
- [ ]
- [ ]

meal planner   wk___

	breakfast	lunch	dinner	snacks
monday				
tuesday				
wednesday				
thursday				
friday				
saturday				
sunday				

shopping list

- [ ]
- [ ]
- [ ]
- [ ]
- [ ]
- [ ]
- [ ]

meal planner wk___

	breakfast	lunch	dinner	snacks
monday				
tuesday				
wednesday				
thursday				
friday				
saturday				
sunday				

shopping list

- [ ]
- [ ]
- [ ]
- [ ]
- [ ]
- [ ]

meal planner   wk___

	breakfast	lunch	dinner	snacks
monday				
tuesday				
wednesday				
thursday				
friday				
saturday				
sunday				

shopping list

- [ ]
- [ ]
- [ ]
- [ ]
- [ ]
- [ ]

meal planner   wk___

	breakfast	lunch	dinner	snacks
monday				
tuesday				
wednesday				
thursday				
friday				
saturday				
sunday				

shopping list

- [ ]
- [ ]
- [ ]
- [ ]
- [ ]
- [ ]

acknowledgements

First of all I want to thank my Editor, Emily North. Em – I'm so grateful for your attention to detail, ideas and encouragement over the last few months. Anika – your amazing design and cover have brought this book to life!

A huge thank you to the Bloomsbury Absolute team – Jon Croft, Meg Boas and Peter Moffat, along with the Bloomsbury London team who were able to see the vision for this book when it was just a concept.

Polly Webster and Adam O'Shepherd – thank you for the wonderful photography and food styling … all done remotely on one of the hottest fortnights on record!

My agent Clare for all your support over the last four years.

My brilliant husband Paul and our boys, Elliot and Sam. I wrote a lot of this book during lockdown. It could have been awful and stressful, but the three of you made it the happiest of times.

To my lovely mum and dad. For your love and support in everything I do.

Thank you to my friends for your endless encouragement – especially Cass, Cro and Fawcus.

I wouldn't have a book if it wasn't for my social media followers. Thank you for all of the messages and support over the last four years. I feel incredibly lucky!

about the author

Amy Sheppard is a busy mum of two boys, living in Cornwall. She was taught to cook by her mum and the key was always making great-tasting food, that didn't cost the earth. Amy has continued cooking in this tradition, developing her own recipes to feed her growing family, focusing on clever meal planning, using up leftovers and sometimes having to get a bit creative with ingredients! Amy now develops recipes for food brands, promoting them to her loyal social media followers @amysheppardfood.

Her first book, *The Savvy Shopper's Cookbook*, was written with busy people in mind, and this, her second book, continues that principle, offering simple, delicious meals that are easy to make, delicious to eat and a joy to cook.

BLOOMSBURY ABSOLUTE
Bloomsbury Publishing Plc
50 Bedford Square, London, WC1B 3DP, UK
29 Earlsfort Terrace, Dublin 2, Ireland

BLOOMSBURY, BLOOMSBURY ABSOLUTE, the Diana logo and the Absolute Press logo are trademarks of Bloomsbury Publishing Plc.

First published in Great Britain 2021.

A catalogue record for this book is available from the British Library.

Library of Congress Cataloguing-in-Publication data has been applied for.

HB: 9781472984647
ePUB: 9781472984623
ePDF: 9781472984616

2 4 6 8 10 9 7 5 3

Printed and bound in China by C&C Offset Printing Co. Ltd.

Bloomsbury Publishing Plc makes every effort to ensure that the papers used in the manufacture of our books are natural, recyclable products made from wood grown in well-managed forests. Our manufacturing processes conform to the environmental regulations of the country of origin.
    To find out more about our authors and books visit www.bloomsbury.com and sign up for our newsletters.

Publisher
Jon Croft

Commissioning Editor
Meg Boas

Design and Art Direction
Anika Schulze
and Peter Moffat

Senior Editor
Emily North

Photography
Polly Webster

Food Styling
Adam O'Shepherd
and Sian Williams

Copyediting
Judy Barratt

Proofreading
Margaret Haynes

Indexing
Zoe Ross